TWELVE SERMONS

ON

THE PRODIGAL SON

AND OTHER TEXTS IN LUKE XV.

BY

C. H. SPURGEON

FLEMING H. REVELL COMPANY

CHICAGO NEW YORK TORONTO

Metropolitan Tabernacle Pulpit.

THE APPROACHABLENESS OF JESUS.

A Sermon

DELIVERED ON SUNDAY EVENING, MAY 3RD, 1868, BY

C. H. SPURGEON,

AT THE METROPOLITAN TABERNACLE, NEWINGTON.

"Then drew near unto him all the publicans and sinners for to hear him."—Luke xv. 1.

THE most depraved and despised classes of society formed an inner ring of nearers around our Lord. I gather from this that he was a most approachable person, that he was not of repulsive manners, but that he courted human confidence and was willing that men should commune with him.

Upon that one thought I shall enlarge, this evening, and may the Holy Spirit make it a loadstone to draw many hearts to Jesus. Eastern monarchs affected great seclusion, and were wont to surround themselves with impassable barriers of state. It was very difficult for even their most loyal subjects to approach them. You remember the case of Esther, who, though the monarch was her husband, yet went with her life in her hand when she ventured to present herself before the king Ahasuerus, for there was a commandment that none should come unto the king except they were called, at peril of their lives. It is not so with the King of kings. His court is far more splendid; his person is far more worshipful; but you may draw near to him at all times without let or hindrance. He hath set no men-at-arms around his palace gate. The door of his house of mercy is set wide open. Over the lintel of his palace gate is written, "For every one that asketh receiveth; and he that seeketh findeth; and to him that knocketh it shall be opened."

Even in our own days great men are not readily to be come at. There are so many back stairs to be climbed before you can reach the official who might have helped you, so many subalterns to be parleyed with, and servants to be passed by, that there is no coming at your object. The good men may be affable enough themselves, but they remind us of the old Russian fable of the hospitable householder in a village, who was willing enough to help all the poor who came to his door, but he kept so many big dogs loose in his yard that nobody was able to get up to the threshold, and therefore his personal affability was of no service to the wanderers. It is not so with our Master. Though he is greater than the greatest, and higher than the highest, he has been pleased to put out of the way everything which might keep the sinner from entering into his halls of gracious entertainment. From his lips we hear no threatenings against intrusion, but hundreds of invitations to the nearest and dearest intimacy. Jesus is to be approached, not now and then, but at all times, and not by some favoured few, but by all in whose hearts his Holy Spirit has enkindled the desire to enter into his secret presence.

The philosophical teachers of our Lord's day affected very great seclusion. They considered their teachings to be so profound and eclectic that they were not to be uttered in the hearing of the common multitude. "Far hence, ye profane," was their scornful motto. Like Simon Stylites, they stood upon a lofty pillar of their fancied self-conceit, and dropped down now and then a stray thought upon the vulgar herd beneath, but they did not condescend to talk familiarly with them, considering it to be a dishonour to their philosophy to communicate it to the multitude. One of the greatest philosophers wrote over his door, "Let no one who is ignorant of geometry enter here;" but our Lord, compared with whom all the wise men are but fools, who is, in fact, the wisdom of God, never drove away a sinner because of his ignorance, never refused a seeker because he was not yet initiated, and had not taken the previous steps in the ladder of learning, and never permitted any thirsty spirit to be chased away from the crystal spring of truth divine. His every word was a diamond, and his lips dropped pearls, but he was never more at home than when speaking to the common people, and teaching them concerning the kingdom of God.

You may thus contrast and compare our Lord's gentle manners with those of kings, and nobles, and sages, but you shall find none to equal him in condescending tenderness. To this attractive quality of our Lord I intend, this evening, as God shall help me, to ask your earnest attention. First, *let us prove it;* secondly, *illustrate it;* and, thirdly, *enforce or improve it.*

I. First, let us PROVE THE APPROACHABLENESS OF CHRIST, though it really needs no proof, for it is a fact which lies upon the surface of his life.

1. You may see it conspicuously *in his offices.* Those offices are too many for us to take them all to-night. We will just cull a handful; say three. Our Lord Jesus is said to be the *Mediator* between God and man. Now, observe, that the office of mediator implies at once that he should be approachable. A daysman, as Job says, is one who can put his hand upon both; but if Jesus will not familiarly put his hand on man, certainly he is no daysman between God and man. A mediator is not a mediator of one—he must be akin to both the parties between whom he mediates. If Jesus Christ shall be a perfect mediator between God and man, he must be able to come to God so near that God shall call him his fellow, and then he must approach to man so closely that he shall not be ashamed to call him brother. This is precisely the case with our Lord. Do think of this, you who are afraid of Jesus. He is a mediator, and as a mediator you may come to him. Jacob's ladder reached from earth to heaven, but if he had cut away half-a-dozen of the bottom rounds, what would have been the good of it? Who could ascend by it into the hill of the Lord? Jesus Christ is the great conjunction between earth and heaven, but if he will not touch the poor mortal man who comes to him, why then, of what service is he

to the sons of men? You do need a mediator between your soul and God; you must not think of coming to God without a mediator; but you do not want any mediator between yourselves and Christ. There is a preparation for coming to God—you must not come to God without a perfect righteousness; but you may come to Jesus without any preparation, and without any righteousness, because as mediator he has in himself all the righteousness and fitness that you require, and is ready to bestow them upon you. You may come boldly to him even now; he waits to reconcile you unto God by his blood.

Another of his offices is that *of priest.* That word "*priest*" has come to smell very badly nowadays; but, for all that, it is a very sweet word as we find it in Holy Scripture. The word "priest" does not mean a gaudily-dressed pretender, who stands apart from other worshippers within the gate, two steps higher than the rest of the people, who professes to have power to dispense pardon for human sin, and I know not what beside. The true priest was truly the brother of all the people. There was no man in the whole camp so brotherly as Aaron. So much were Aaron and the priests who succeeded him the first points of contact with men, on God's behalf, that when a leper had become too unclean for anybody else to draw near to him, the last man who touched him was the priest. The house might be leprous, but the priest went into it, and the man might be leprous, but he talked with him, and examined him, the last of Israel's tribes who might be familiar with the wretched outcast; and if afterwards that diseased man was cured, the first person who touched him must be a priest. "Go, show thyself to the priest," was the command, to every recovering leper; and until the priest had entered into fellowship with him, and had given him a certificate of health, he could not be received into the Jewish camp. The priest was the true brother of the people, chosen from among themselves, at all times to be approached; living in their midst, in the very centre of the camp, ready to make intercession for the sinful and the sorrowful. So is it with our Lord. I read just now, in your hearing, that he can be touched with a feeling of our infirmities, and that he was tempted in all points like as we are, yet without sin. Surely, you will never doubt that if Jesus perfectly sustains the office of priest, as he certainly does, he must be the most approachable of beings, approachable by the poor sinner, who has given himself up to despair, whom only a sacrifice can save; approachable by the foul harlot who is put outside the camp, whom only the blood can cleanse; approachable by the miserable thief who has to suffer the punishment of his crimes, whom only the great High Priest can absolve. No other man may care to touch you, O trembling outcast, but Jesus will. You may be separated from all of human kind, justly and righteously, by your iniquities, but you are not separated from that great Friend of sinners who at this very time is willing that publicans and sinners should draw near unto him.

As a third office let me mention that *the Lord Jesus is our Saviour;* but I see not how he can be a Saviour unless he can be approached by those who need to be saved. The priest and the Levite passed by on the other side when the bleeding man lay in the road to Jericho; they were not saviours, therefore, and could not be, but he was the saviour who came where the man was, stooped over him, and took wine and oil and poured them into the gaping fissures of his wounds, and lifted him up with tender love and set him on his own beast, and led him to the inn. He was the true saviour; and, O sinner, Jesus Christ will come just where you are, and your wounds of sin, even though they are putrid, shall not drive him away from you. His love shall overcome the nauseating offensiveness of your iniquity, for he is able and willing to save such as you are. I might mention many other of the offices of Christ, but these three will suffice. Certainly if the Spirit blesses them, you will be led to see that Jesus is not hard to reach.

2. Consider a few of his *names and titles*. Frequently Jesus is called the "*Lamb*." Blessed name! I do not suppose there is any one here who was ever afraid of a lamb; that little girl yonder, if she saw a lamb, would not be frightened. Every child seems almost instinctively to long to put its hand on the head of a lamb. O that you might come and put your hand on the head of Christ, the Lamb of God that taketh away the sin of the world.

"Oh see how Jesus trusts himself
Unto our childish love,
As though by his free ways with us
Our earnestness to prove!

His sacred name a common word
On earth he loves to hear;
There is no majesty in him
Which love may not come near."

Again, you find him called a *Shepherd:* no one is afraid of a shepherd. If you were travelling in the East, and you saw Bedouins or Turkish soldiery in the distance, you might be alarmed; but if some one said, "Oh, it is only a few shepherds," you would not be afraid of them. The sheep are not at all timid when near the shepherd. O poor wandering sheep, you, perhaps, have come to be afraid of Christ, but there is no reason why you should be, for this heavenly Shepherd says, "I will seek out my sheep, and will deliver them out of all places where they have been scattered in the cloudy and dark day."

"See Israel's gentle Shepherd stands
With all engaging charms."

Timid, foolish, and wandering though you may be, there is nothing in the good Shepherd to drive you away from him, but everything to entice you to come to him. Then, again, he is called our *Brother*, and one always feels that he may approach his brother. I have no thought of trouble or distress which I would hesitate to communicate to my brother here, for he is so good and kind. I do not think I could be in any trouble which I should not expect him to do his best to help me out of. I never feel that there is any distance between him and me, nor do you, I hope, feel so with regard to your brothers. Even so, is it with this Brother born for adversity. Believer, how is it that you are sometimes so backward and so cold towards Jesus? Christ is approachable.

"The light of love is round his feet,
His paths are never dim;
And he comes nigh to us when we
Dare not come nigh to him."

You need not think that your troubles are too trifling to bring to him; he has an open ear for the little daily vexations of life. Brethren, you can come to the good elder Brother at all hours; and when he blames you for coming, let me know. He is called, too, a *Friend;* but he would be a very unfriendly friend who could not be approached by those he professed to love. If my friend puts a hedge around himself, and holds himself so very dignified that I may not speak with him, I would rather be without his friendship; but if he be a genuine friend, and I stand at his door knocking, he will say, "Come in, and welcome; what can I do for you?" Such a friend is Jesus Christ. He is to be met with by all needy, seeking hearts.

3. There is room enough for enlargement here, but I have no time to say more, therefore I will give you another plea. *Recollect his person.* The person of our Lord Jesus Christ proclaims this truth with a trumpet voice. I say his person, because he is man, born of woman, bone of our bone, and flesh of our flesh. The Lord Jesus Christ is God, but if he were God only, you might well stand at a distance, and shudder at the splendour of his majesty. But he is man as well as God, and so it comes to pass, as Dr. Watts puts it—

"Till God in human flesh I see,
My thoughts no comfort find;
The holy, just, and sacred Three
Are terrors to my mind.

But if Immanuel's face appear,
My hope, my joy begins;
His name forbids my slavish fear,
His grace removes my sins."

When I see Christ in the manger where the horned ox fed, or hanging on a woman's breast, or obedient to his parents, or "a Man of sorrows and acquainted with grief," a poor man without a place whereon to lay his head, then I feel that I can freely come to him. Think of him as being precisely such as you are, in all and everything except sin, and then you will never have a thought that he will chide you for drawing near, or drive you away when you venture to supplicate him. But I want especially to say to you that if you could but see my Master's person as he was when here on earth, you would have henceforth and for ever the thought that you might not come to him expelled from your mind. I know not what may have been his beauties, or what may have been the appearance of his lovely countenance, but of this I am persuaded, that if he could but come here to-night, and I could vacate this platform for him whose shoe-latchet I am not worthy to unloose, you who groan under a sense of unworthiness would not run away. If Moses stood here with his flaming countenance, you would shade your eyes, and ask that if you must look upon him he might wear a veil; but if Christ were here, oh! how you longing seeking ones would gaze upon him! There would be no drooping of the eyelids, no covering of the face, no alarm, no anguish—his face is too sweet for that. And if the Master should walk down the aisles, the most timid of you would long to touch the hem of his garment and to kiss the floor whereon he had set his feet. I know you would not fear to look into that face.

And then that voice, how would you be charmed, you poor trembling seekers, if you heard him say, "Take my yoke upon you, and learn of me;" you would discover such meekness and lowliness in him, that you would not think of starting back. Oh! if your eyes could but see him, I feel persuaded that, graciously drawn by his charms, your hearts would hasten to him. Well, believer, come to him, come to him; come close to him. Come with your troubles and tell him all about them. Come with your sins and ask to have them washed away anew.

"Let us be simple with him, then,
Not backward, stiff, or cold,
As though our Bethlehem could be
What Sina was of old."

And you, poor trembling sinner, come to him; come to him now, for he has said, "Him that cometh to me I will in no wise cast out." Oh! if your eyes were opened to behold him, you would perceive that the glory of his person lies not in the splendour which repels, but in the majesty which divinely attracts.

4. If this suffice not, *let me here remind you of the language of Christ*, He proclaims his approachability in such words as these, "Come unto me, all ye that labour and are heavy laden, and I will give you rest." Ye horny-handed sons of toil, ye smiths and carpenters, ye ploughers and diggers, come unto me, yea, come all ye that labour and are heavy laden, and I will give you rest. And again, "If any man thirst, let him come unto me and drink." He invites men to come; he pleads with them to come; and when they will not come he gently upbraids them with such words as these, "Ye will not come unto me that ye might have life." And, again, "O Jerusalem, Jerusalem, thou that killest the prophets, and stonest them which are sent unto thee, how often would I have gathered thy children together, even as a hen gathereth her chickens under her wings, *and ye would not.*" It is not "*I* would not," but "*ye* would not." Why, the whole of Scripture in its invitations, may be said to be the language of Christ, and therein you find loving, pleading words of this kind, "Come now, and let us reason together: though your sins be as scarlet, they shall be as white as snow; though they be red like crimson, they shall be as wool." "Let the wicked forsake his way, and the unrighteous man his thoughts: and let him return unto the Lord, and he will have mercy upon him; and to our God, for he will abundantly pardon." All our blessed Lord's sermons were so many loving calls to poor aching hearts to come and find what they needed in him. I pray that the Holy Spirit may give an effectual call to many of you to-night. It would glad the heart of the Redeemer in the skies if you would come to him for salvation, for you may come, since there is no barrier between you and the Saviour of men. What is it keeps you back? I repeat it with tears, what is it keeps you back?

The old proverb truly saith that "actions speak louder than words," and therefore let us review the general ways and manners of the Redeemer. You may gather that he is the most approachable of persons *from the actions of his life*. He was always very busy, and busy about the most important of matters, and yet he never shut the door in the face of any applicant. Her Majesty's cabinet have to discuss most important political matters just now, but compared with the work which filled the Saviour's hands and heart, their discussions are mere trifles. Our Master might well have claimed seclusion, but he did not. He sought it but he found none, save only at midnight, when he watched and prayed. No sort of appeal for audience did Jesus frown upon. There were certain mothers in the land, poor simple-minded women, and they took it into their heads one day that they would like to have the Master's hands put upon the heads of their little ones. So they came, bringing their boys and girls, but some of the disciples said, "The Master must not be disturbed by children; go ye your ways, and take your children back." But what said he? How different from his followers! he rebuked their harshness, and said, "Suffer the little children to come unto me, for of such is the kingdom of heaven." You see he is a child's friend. Dear young people, think of that. Jesus does not drive you away, but though he is so great and glorious that all the angels of God worship him, yet he stoops to hear the prayers and praises of little children. Seek him now, for those who seek him early shall find him. Let me tell you another story. There was a woman in the city who was a sinner. You know the meaning, the dark sad meaning of that title in her case; I need not explain that. Poor soul! Her sin had caused her to be despised and shunned by everyone, but she had been forgiven, and in gratitude she poured the precious ointment on her beloved Saviour's feet, and then wiped them with the hairs of her head; and when the Pharisee Simon would have had her rebuked, the loving Master said, "She loves much because she has had much forgiven." He is approachable by all, then, even by the worst; even the harlot need not fear to draw near to him—his touch can make her pure. I have noted one thing in Christ's life, and noted it with delight. Our Lord was always preaching, and he often grew weary, as we do, and therefore he wanted a little retirement, but the multitude came breaking in upon his solitude, following him on foot when he had sailed away to escape them; this was troublesome, and to us it would have been irritating, yet he never uttered an angry, fretful syllable. There was no rest for him, because of the eager crowd; but did he ever say, "How these people tease me; how they worry me"? No, never; his big heart made him forget himself. He was approachable to all at all hours; even his meals were disturbed, but he was gentle towards those thoughtless intruders. Not once was he harsh and repulsive. His whole life proves the truth of the prophecy, "The bruised reed he will not break, and the smoking flax he will not quench." He graciously receives the weak and the feeble ones who come to him, and sends none empty away.

6. But, if you want the crowning argument, look yonder. The man who has lived a life of service, at last dies a felon's death! Look upon his head girt with the crown of thorns! Mark well his cheeks whence they have plucked off the hair! See the spittle from those scornful mouths, staining his marred countenance! Mark the crimson rivers which are flowing from his back where they have scourged him! See his hands and his feet which are pierced with the nails, and from which ensanguined rills are flowing! Look to that face so full of anguish, listen to his cry, "I thirst, I thirst;" and as you see him there expiring, can you think that he will spurn the seeker? As you see him turn

his head and say to the dying thief by his side, "To-day shalt thou be with me in paradise," you dare not belie him so much as to deem that you may not come to him. You will outrage your reason if you start back from Jesus crucified. The cross of Christ should be the centre to which all hearts are drawn, the focus of desire, the pivot of hope, the anchorage of faith. You may come, sinner, black, vile, hellish sinner, you may come and have life even as the dying thief had it when he said, "Lord, remember me."

"There is life in a look at the crucified One."

Surely, you need not be afraid to come to him who went to Calvary for sinners. Why linger? Why hesitate? Why those blushes, sobs, and tears?

"Why art thou afraid to come,
And tell him all thy case?
He will not pronounce thy doom,
Nor frown thee from his face.
Wilt thou fear Immanuel?
Or dread the Lamb of God,
Who, to save thy soul from hell,
Has shed his precious blood?"

Did I hear a whisper, did anybody say that Christ is now in heaven, and that he may have changed? Ah, groundless insinuation! Do you know what he is doing in heaven at this moment? He is exalted on high to give repentance and remission of sins. What a help that is to those who are coming to him! This repentance is the greatest want of coming sinners, and he from the skies supplies it. Moreover, "he ever liveth to make intercession for us." His occupation in the skies is to plead for those sinners whom he redeemed with his blood, and hence he is able to save them unto the uttermost. Since he is the intercessor for souls, there is no reason why you should start back, but every reason why you should boldly come to the throne of the heavenly grace, because you have a High Priest who is passed into the heavens.

"Compell'd by bleeding love,
Ye wandering sheep draw near;
Christ calls you from above—
His charming accents hear!
Let whosoever will now come,
In mercy's breast there still is room."

Here I leave this part of the subject. Some of you little know how heavily this sermon is hanging on my mind. I preach my very soul to you this day. I wish I knew how to preach so as to win some of you for my Lord, this evening; I should be glad to go even to the school of affliction if I might learn to preach more successfully. But I can do no more. May the Eternal Spirit, in answer to the prayers of his people, which I hope are going up now, be pleased to make you feel the sweet attractions of the cross of Christ, and may you come to him, so that it may be said again to-night, "Then drew near unto him publicans and sinners."

II. I now shall proceed, with as great brevity as I can command, TO ILLUSTRATE THIS GREAT TRUTH.

I illustrate it, in the first place, by *the way which Christ opens up for sinners to himself.* What is the way for a sinner to come to Christ? It is simply this—the sinner, feeling his need of a Saviour, trusts himself to the Lord Jesus Christ. This was the perplexity of my boyhood, but it is so simple now. When I was told to go to Christ, I thought "Yes, if I knew where he was, I would go to him—no matter how I wearied myself, I would trudge on till I found him." I never could understand how I could get to Christ till I understood that it is a mental coming, a spiritual coming, a coming with the mind. The coming to Jesus which saves the soul is a simple reliance upon him, and if, to-night, being sensible of your guilt, you will rely upon the atoning blood of Jesus, you have come to him, and you are saved. Is he not, then, approachable indeed, if there is so simple a way of coming? No good works, ceremonies, or experiences are demanded, a childlike faith is the royal road to Jesus.

This truth is further illustrated by *the help which he gives to coming sinners, in order to bring them near to himself.* He it is who first makes them coming sinners. It is his Eternal Spirit who draws them unto himself. They would not come to him of themselves, they are without desires towards him, but it is his work to cast secret silken cords around their hearts, which he draws with his strong hand, and brings them near to himself. Depend upon it, he will never refuse those whom he himself draws by his Spirit. Rest assured he will never shut the door in the face of any soul that comes to feed at the gospel banquet, moved to approach by the power of his love. He said once, "Compel them to come in," but he never said, "Shut the door in their faces and bolt them out."

I might further illustrate this to the children of God, *by reminding you of the way in which you now commune with your Lord.* How easy it is for you to reach his ear and his heart! A prayer, a sigh, a tear, a groan, will admit you into the King's chambers. You may be in a very sad frame of mind, but when you come to him, how soon he makes your soul like the chariots of Ammi-nadib. Dark may be your midnight, but as soon as you draw nigh to him your night is over. "He giveth liberally, and upbraideth not." While he acts thus with you, the sinner may very well believe that he will receive him too.

The approachableness of Christ may also be seen in the fact *of his receiving the poor offerings of his people.* The very holiest deeds which you and I can do for Christ are poor and faulty at the best. As I sat studying at my table last night, there was before me a little withered flower—a sprig of wall-flower—which has been lying for some weeks on my table. It comes from a very, very poor child of God, many miles away, who gets a blessing from reading my sermons, and she has nothing in the world besides to give me, but she sends me this flower, and I value it because it is a token of Christian affection and gratitude. So is it with our Master. The very best sermons that we preach, and the largest contributions we give to his treasury, are only just like that poor little withered wall-flower; but the Master puts our service in his bosom, and keeps it there, and thinks much of it because he loves us. Does not that prove how generous, how condescending, how tender he must be? Believe him to be so, ye fearful souls, and come to him.

The ordinances wear upon their forefront the impress of an ever approachable Saviour. Baptism in outward type sets forth our fellowship with him in his death, burial, and resurrection—what can be nearer than this? The Lord's supper in visible symbol invites us to eat his flesh and drink his blood: this reveals to us most clearly how welcome we are to the most intimate intercourse with Jesus. The heaven of heavens shall afford us yet another illustration. There are tens of thousands now in the skies who came to Jesus just as they were, in all the filth and *deshabille* of the lost estate, and he received every one of them into his heart of love and arms of power. There are many thousands on earth, there are some thousands now in this Tabernacle, who can testify that they have found Jesus to be a very tender and generous friend. Now, if he has received us, why should he not receive you? Be encouraged to believe that inasmuch as he has received others he has open arms for you also.

Let me joyfully remind you that *Jesus never has rejected a seeking sinner*. There is not to be found in all the kingdoms of the universe a single instance of a sincere seeker after Christ being cast away, and there never shall be, for he hath not said to the seed of Jacob, "Seek ye my face in vain," but he has said, "Him that cometh to me I will in no wise cast out." Beloved, if there had been a single soul cast away we should have known of it by now. It is eighteen hundred and sixty-eight years now, and if a solitary penitent had been rejected, we should have heard of it before now, for I will tell you of one who would have spread it abroad, and that is the devil. If he could get a single instance of a soul who had repented and trusted Christ, but found that Christ would have nothing to do with him, it would be a standing scandal against the cross which Satan would delight to publish. I know, poor sinners, what the devil will tell you when you are coming to Christ—he will describe Jesus as a hard master, but do you tell him he is a liar from the beginning, and a murderer, and that he is trying to murder your soul by making you swallow his poisonous lies.

III. In the third place, we come TO ENFORCE THIS TRUTH; or, as the old Puritans used to say, improve it.

The first enforcement I give is this: let those of us who are working for the Master in soul-winning, *try to be like Christ in this matter*, and not be, as some are apt to be, proud, stuck-up, distant, or formal. Oh, dear, dear! the lofty ministerial airs that one has seen assumed by men who ought to have been meek and lowly. What a grand set of men some of the preachers of the past age thought themselves to be! I trust those who played the archbishop have nearly all gone to heaven, but a few linger among us who use little grace and much starch. The grand divines never shook hands with anybody, except, indeed, with the deacons, and a little knot of evidently superior persons. Amongst

Dissenters it was almost as bad as it is in most church congregations, where you feel that the good man, by his manner, is always saying, "I hope you know who I am, Sir; I am the rector of the parish." Now, all that kind of stuck-upishness is altogether wrong. No man can do good in that way; and no good at all comes of assuming superiority and distance. The best teacher for boys is the man who can make himself a boy; and the best teacher for girls is the woman who can make herself a girl among girls. I often regret that I have so large a congregation; you will say, "Why?" Why, when I had a smaller congregation at Park Street, there were too many even then, but I did get a shake of the hand sometimes; but now there are so many of you that I scarcely know you, good memory as I have, and I seldom have the pleasure of shaking hands with you—I wish I did. If there is anybody in the wide world whose good I wish to promote, it is yours; therefore I wish to be at home with you: and if ever I should affect the airs of a great man, and set myself above you all, and separate myself by proud manners from your sympathy, I hope the Lord will take me down and make me right again. We may expect souls to be saved when we do as Christ did, namely, get publicans and sinners to draw near to us. Now, that is a practical point which, though you have smiled about it, will not I hope be forgotten by you.

There is this to be said to you who are unconverted—if Jesus Christ be so approachable, oh! *how I wish, how I wish that you would approach him.* There are no bolts upon his doors, no barred iron gates to pass, no big dogs to keep you back. If Christ be so approachable by all needy ones, then needy one, come, and welcome. Come just now! What is it keeps you back? You think that you do not feel your need enough, or that you are not fit to come—both of which suspicions are selfrighteousness in different shapes. O that you did know but your need of Jesus, in order to be able even to do so much as feel your need. You are a poor, miserable bankrupt before God, and Christ alone can enrich you. Do not talk of fitness; there is no such thing:—

"All the fitness he requireth,
Is to feel your need of him:
This he gives you;
'Tis the Spirit's rising beam."

Come, then. There is such mercy to be had; there is such a hell to be escaped from; there is such a heaven to be opened for you; delay not, but believe at once. Come, come, come!

"Come, and welcome;
Come, and welcome, sinner, come!"

I stand at mercy's door to-night, and say to every passer-by, in the name of the Master, "My oxen and fatlings are killed; come, come, come to the supper!" O that you would come this very night!

Some of us are coming to the Lord's table to celebrate his love because we have first come to himself. I do not ask you who are not saved to come to that table—you ought not to come; you must first come to Jesus, and then you may come to this ordinance. Meanwhile, the best thing you can do is to come to Christ, and let me ask you to remember this, that in proportion as Christ is accessible, so your guilt will be increased if you do not come to him. If it be easy to come to him, what excuse can there be for you if you refuse to accept him? I have tried to tell you what the way of salvation is. If I knew how to use better language, or even coarser language, if that would suit you, it should be alike to me if I might but touch your consciences, break your hearts, and bring you to Christ. But I protest before you that if you will not come to my Master, I can do no more. I shall be clear of your blood at the last, and in the day of judgment your ruin must be upon your own heads. But let it not be so. Jesus bids you come. O you needy ones, let your need impel you to come at once, that you may find eternal life in him.

The last word is—if Jesus be such a Saviour as we have described him, *let saints and sinners join to praise him.* How marvellous that our dear Lord should be so condescending to us unworthy ones as to come all the way from heaven to earth for us! Oh, matchless love that made him stoop to grief and death! Oh, unspeakable condescension, to come thus to poor sinners' hearts, bearing mercies in both his hands, and freely giving them to undeserving rebels! For this unspeakable grace let us praise him! You who are coming to his table, draw near with praises in your mouths. Come praising the condescending love in which *you* have participated, and which has saved you from eternal death. Even you who sit as spectators, I do trust will have your mind filled with grateful thoughts.

"Jesus sits on Zion's hill;
He receives poor sinners still.

Blessed be his name, world without end!

Metropolitan Tabernacle Pulpit.

THE PARABLE OF THE LOST SHEEP.

A Sermon

DELIVERED ON LORD'S-DAY MORNING, SEPTEMBER 28TH, 1884, BY

C. H. SPURGEON,

AT THE METROPOLITAN TABERNACLE, NEWINGTON.

"What man of you, having an hundred sheep, if he lose one of them, doth not leave the ninety and nine in the wilderness, and go after that which is lost, until he find it? And when he hath found it, he layeth it on his shoulders, rejoicing. And when he cometh home, he calleth together his friends and neighbours, saying unto them, Rejoice with me; for I have found my sheep which was lost. I say unto you, that likewise joy shall be in heaven over one sinner that repenteth, more than over ninety and nine just persons, which need no repentance."—Luke xv. 4—7

OUR Lord Jesus Christ while he was here below was continually in the pursuit of lost souls. He was seeking lost men and women, and it was for this reason that he went down among them, even among those who were most evidently lost, that he might find them. He took pains to put himself where he could come into communication with them, and he exhibited such kindliness towards them that in crowds they drew near to hear him. I dare say it was a queer-looking assembly, a disreputable rabble, which made the Lord Jesus its centre. I am not astonished that the Pharisee, when he looked upon the congregation, sneered and said, "He collects around him the pariahs of our community, the wretches who collect taxes for the foreigner of God's free people; and the fallen women of the towns, and such-like riffraff make up his audiences; and he, instead of repelling them, receives them, welcomes them, looks upon them as a class to whom he has a peculiar relationship. He even eats with them. Did he not go into the house of Zaccheus, and the house of Levi, and partake of the feasts which these low people made for him?" We cannot tell you all the Pharisees thought, it might not be edifying to attempt it; but they thought as badly of the Lord as they possibly could, because of the company which surrounded him. And so, he deigns in this parable to defend himself; not that he cared much about what they might think, but that they might have no excuse for speaking so bitterly of him. He tells them that he was seeking the lost, and where should he be found but among those whom he was seeking? Should a physician shun the sick? Should a shepherd avoid the lost sheep? Was he not exactly in his right position when there "drew near unto him all the publicans and sinners for to hear him"?

Our divine Lord defended himself by what is called an *argumentum ad hominem*, an argument to the men themselves; for he said, "What man *of you*, having an hundred sheep, if he lose one of them, doth not go after that which is lost, until he find it?" No argument tells more powerfully upon men than one which comes close home to their own daily life, and the Saviour put it so. They were silenced, if they were not convinced. It was a peculiarly strong argument, because in their case it was only a sheep that they would go after, but in his case it was something infinitely more precious than all the flocks of sheep that ever fed on Sharon or Carmel; for it was the soul of man which he sought to save. The argument had in it not only the point of peculiar adaptation, but a force at the back of it unusually powerful for driving it home upon every honest mind. It may be opened out in this fashion,—"If you men would each one of you go after a lost sheep, and follow in its track until you found it, how much more may I go after lost souls, and follow them in all their wanderings until I can rescue them?" The going after the sheep is a part of the parable which our Lord meant them to observe: the shepherd pursues a route which he would never think of pursuing if it were only for his own pleasure; his way is not selected for his own ends, but for the sake of the stray sheep. He takes a track up hill and down dale, far into a desert, or into some dark wood, simply because the sheep has gone that way, and he must follow it until he find it. Our Lord Jesus Christ, as a matter of taste and pleasure, would never have been found among the publicans and sinners, nor among any of our guilty race: if he had consulted his own ease and comfort he would have consorted only with pure and holy angels, and the great Father above; but he was not thinking of himself, his heart was set upon the lost ones, and therefore he went where the lost sheep were; "for the Son of man is come to seek and to save that which was lost." The more steadily you look at this parable the more clearly you will see that our Lord's answer was complete. We need not this morning regard it exclusively as an answer to Pharisees, but we may look at it as an instruction to ourselves; for it is quite as complete in that direction. May the good Spirit instruct us as we muse upon it.

I. In the first place, I call attention to this observation: THE ONE SUBJECT OF THOUGHT to the man who had lost his sheep. This sets forth to us the one thought of our Lord Jesus Christ, the Good Shepherd, when he sees a man lost to holiness and happiness by wandering into sin.

The shepherd, on looking over his little flock of one hundred, can only count ninety-nine. He counts them again, and he notices that a certain one has gone: it may be a white-faced sheep with a black mark on its foot: he knows all about it, for "the Lord knoweth them that are his." The shepherd has a photograph of the wanderer in his mind's eye, and now he thinks but little of the ninety and nine who are feeding in the pastures of the wilderness, but his mind is in a ferment about the one lost sheep. This one idea possesses him: "a sheep is lost!" This agitates his mind more and more—"a sheep is lost." It masters his every faculty. He cannot eat bread; he cannot return to his home; he cannot rest while one sheep is lost.

To a tender heart a lost sheep is a painful subject of thought. It is a sheep, and therefore utterly *defenceless* now that it has left its defender. If the wolf should spy it out, or the lion or the bear should come across its track, it would be torn in pieces in an instant. Thus the shepherd asks his heart the question—"What will become of my sheep? Perhaps at this very moment a lion may be ready to spring upon it, and, if so, it cannot help itself!" A sheep is not prepared for fight, and even for flight it has not the swiftness of its enemy. That makes its compassionate owner the more sad as he thinks again—"A sheep is lost, it is in great danger of a cruel death." A sheep is of all creatures the most *senseless.* If we have lost a dog, it may find its way home again; possibly a horse might return to its master's stable; but a sheep will wander on and on, in endless mazes lost. It is too foolish a thing to think of returning to the place of safety. A lost sheep is lost indeed in countries where lands lie unenclosed and the plains are boundless. That fact still seems to ring in the man's soul—"A sheep is lost, and it will not return, for it is a foolish thing. Where may it not have gone by this time? Weary and worn, it may be fainting; it may be far away from green pastures, and be ready to perish with hunger among the bare rocks or upon the arid sand." A sheep is *shiftless;* it knows nothing about providing for itself. The camel can scent water from afar, and a vulture can espy its food from an enormous distance; but the sheep can find nothing for itself. Of all wretched creatures a lost sheep is one of the worst. If anybody had stepped up to the shepherd just then, and said, "Good sir, what aileth you? you seem in great concern"; he would have replied, "And well I may be, for a sheep is lost." "It is only one, sir; and I see you have ninety-nine left." "Do you call it nothing to lose one? You are no shepherd yourself, or you would not trifle so. Why, I seem to forget these ninety-nine that are all safe, and my mind only remembers that one which is lost."

What is it which makes the Great Shepherd lay so much to his heart the loss of one of his flock? What is it that makes him agitated as he reflects upon that supposition—"if he lose one of them"?

I think it is, first, because of *his property in it.* The parable does not so much speak of a hired shepherd, but of a shepherd proprietor. "What man of you having an hundred sheep, if he lose one of them." Jesus, in another place, speaks of the hireling, whose own the sheep are not, and therefore he flees when the wolf comes. It is the shepherd proprietor who lays down his life for the sheep. It is not a sheep alone, and a lost sheep, but it is one of his own lost sheep that this man cares for. This parable is not written about lost humanity in the bulk—it may be so used if you please—but in its first sense it is written about Christ's own sheep; as also is the second parable concerning the woman's own money; and the third, not concerning any prodigal youth, but the father's own son. Jesus has his own sheep, and some of them are lost: yea, they were all once in the same condition; for "all we like sheep have gone astray; we have turned every one to his own way." The parable refers to the unconverted, whom Jesus has redeemed with his most precious blood, and whom he has undertaken to seek and to save: these are those other sheep whom also he must bring in. "For thus saith the Lord God; Behold I, even I, will both search my sheep, and seek them out. As a shepherd seeketh out his flock in the day that he is among his sheep that are scattered; so will I seek out my sheep, and will deliver them out of all places where they have been scattered in the cloudy and dark day." The sheep of Christ are his long before they know it—his even when they wander; and when they are brought into the fold by the effectual working of his grace they become manifestly what they were in covenant from of old. The sheep are Christ's, first, because he chose them from before the foundations of the world—"Ye have not chosen me, but I have chosen you." His, next, because the Father gave them to him. How he dwells upon that fact in his great prayer in John xvii.: "Thine they were, and thou gavest them me;" "Father, I will that they also, whom thou hast given me, be with me where I am." We are the Lord's own flock, furthermore, by his purchase of us; he says: "I lay down my life for the sheep." It is nearly nineteen centuries ago since he paid the ransom price, and bought us to be his own; and we shall be his, for that purchase-money was not paid in vain. And so the Saviour looks upon his hands, and sees the marks of his purchase; he looks upon his side, and sees the token of the effectual redemption of his own elect unto himself by the pouring out of his own heart's blood before the living God. This thought, therefore, presses upon him, "One of my sheep is lost." It is a wonderful supposition, that which is contained in this parable—"if he lose one of them." What! lose one whom he loved or ever the earth was? It may wander for a time, but he will not have it lost for ever: that he cannot bear. What! lose one whom his Father gave him to be his own? Lose one whom he has bought with his own life? He will not endure the thought. That word—"if he lose one of them" sets his soul on fire. It shall not be. You know how much the Lord has valued each one of his chosen, laying down his life for his redemption. You know how dearly he loves every one of his people: it is no new passion with him, neither can it grow old. He has loved his own and must love them to the end. From eternity that love has endured already, and it must continue throughout the ages, for he changeth not. Will he lose one of those so dearly loved? Never; never. He has eternal possession of them by a covenant of salt, wherein the Father hath given them to him: this it is which in great measure stirs his soul so that he thinks of nothing but this fact,—One of my sheep is lost.

Secondly, he has yet another reason for this all-absorbing thought, namely, *his great compassion* for his lost sheep. The wandering of a soul causes Jesus deep sorrow; he cannot bear the thought of its perishing. Such is the love and tenderness of his heart that he cannot bear that one of his own should he in jeopardy. He can take no rest as long as a soul for whom he shed his blood still abides under the dominion of Satan and under the power of sin; therefore the Great Shepherd neither night nor day forgetteth his sheep: he must save his flock, and he is straitened till it be accomplished.

He has a deep sympathy with each stray heart. He knows the sorrow that sin brings, the deep pollution and the terrible wounding that comes of transgression, even at the time; and the sore heart and the broken spirit that will come of it before long; and so the sympathetic Saviour grieves over each lost sheep, for he knows the misery which lies in the fact of being lost. If you have ever been in a house with a mother and father, and daughters and sons, when a little child has been lost, you will never forget the agitation of each member of the household. See the father as he goes to the police-station, and calls at every likely house; for he must find his child or break his heart. See the deep oppression and bitter anguish of the mother; she is like one distracted till she has news of her darling. You now begin to understand what Jesus feels for one whom he loves, who is graven on the palms of his hands, whom he looked upon in the glass of his foreknowledge, when he was bleeding his life away upon the tree; he hath no rest in his spirit till his beloved is found. He hath compassion like a God, and that doth transcend all the compassion of parents or of brothers,—the compassion of an infinite heart brimming over with an ocean of love. This one thought moves the pity of the Lord—"if he lose one of them."

Moreover, the man in the parable had a third relation to the sheep, which made him possessed with the one thought of its being lost,—*he was a shepherd to it.* It was his own sheep, and he had therefore for that very reason become its shepherd; and he says to himself, "If I lose one of them my shepherd-work will be ill-done." What dishonour it would be to a shepherd to lose one of his sheep! Either it must be for want of power to keep it, or want of will, or want of watchfulness; but none of these can appertain to the Chief Shepherd. Our Lord Jesus Christ will never have it said of him that he has lost one of his people, for he glories in having preserved them all. "While I was with them in the world, I kept them in thy name: those that thou gavest me I have kept, and none of them is lost, but the son of perdition; that the scripture might be fulfilled." The devil shall never say that Jesus suffered one whom his Father gave him to perish. His work of love cannot in any degree become a failure. His death in vain! No, not in jot or tittle. I can imagine, if it were possible, that the Son of God should live in vain: but to die in vain! It shall never be. The purpose that he meant to achieve by his passion and death he shall achieve, for he is the Eternal, the Infinite, the Omnipotent; and who shall stay his hand, or baffle his design? He will not have it. "If he lose one of them," says the passage; imagine the consequence. What scorn would come from Satan! What derision would he pour upon the Shepherd! How hell would ring with the news, "He hath lost one of them." Suppose it to be the feeblest; then would they cry, "He could keep the strong, who could keep themselves." Suppose it to be the strongest; then would they cry, "He could not even keep one of the mightiest of them, but must needs let him perish." This is good argument, for Moses pleaded with God, "What will the Egyptians say?" It is not the will of your Father which is in heaven that one of these little ones shall perish, neither is it for the glory of Christ that one of his own sheep should be eternally lost.

You see the reason for the Lord's heart being filled with one burning thought; for first, the sheep is his own; next, he is full of compassion; and then again, it is his office to shepherd the flock.

All this while the sheep is not thinking about the shepherd, or caring for him in the least degree. Some of you are not thinking at all about the Lord Jesus. You have no wish nor will to seek after him! What folly! Oh, the pity of it, that the great heart above should be yearning over you to-day, and should fail to rest because you are in peril, and you, who will be the greater loser, for you will lose your own soul, are sporting with sin, and making yourself merry with destruction. Ah, me! how far you have wandered! How hopeless would your case be if there were not an Almighty Shepherd to think upon you.

II. Now we come to the second point, and observe THE ONE OBJECT OF SEARCH. This sheep lies on the shepherd's heart, and he must at once set out to look for it. He leaves the ninety-and-nine in the wilderness, and goes after that which is lost until he find it.

Observe here that it is *a definite search*. The shepherd goes after the sheep, and after nothing else; and he has the one particular sheep in his mind's eye. I should have imagined, from the way in which I have seen this text handled, that Christ, the Shepherd, went down into the wilderness to catch anybody's sheep he could find. Many were running about, and he did not own any one of them more than another, but was content to pick up the one that he could first lay hold upon; or rather, that which first came running after him. Not so is the case depicted in the parable. It is his own sheep that he is seeking, and he goes distinctly after that one. It is his sheep which was lost,—a well-known sheep; well known not only to himself, but even to his friends and neighbours,—for he speaks to them as if it was perfectly understood which sheep it was that he went to save. Jesus knows all about his redeemed, and he goes definitely after such and such a soul. When I am preaching in the name of the Lord, I delight to think that I am sent to individuals with the message of mercy. I am not going to draw the bow at a venture at all; but when the Divine hands are put on mine to draw the bow, the Lord takes such aim that no arrow misses its mark: into the very centre of the heart the word finds its way; for Jesus goes not forth at a peradventure in his dealings with men. He subdues the will and conquers the heart, making his people willing in the day of his power. He calls individuals and they come. He saith, "Mary," and the response is, "Rabboni." I say, the man in the parable sought out a distinct individual, and rested not till he found it; and so doth the Lord Jesus in the movements of his love go forth at no uncertainty: he does not grope about to catch whom he may, as if he played at Blindman's-buff with salvation, but he seeks and saves the one out of his own sheep which he has his eye upon in its wanderings. Jesus knows what he means to do, and he will perform it to the glory of the Father.

Note that this is *an all-absorbing search*. He is thinking of nothing but his own lost sheep. The ninety-and-nine are left in safety; but they *are* left. When we read that he leaves them in the wilderness we are apt to think of some barren place; but that is not intended: it simply means the open pasturage, the steppe, the prairie: he leaves them well provided for, leaves them because he can leave them. For the time being he is carried away with the one thought that he must seek and save the lost one, and therefore he leaves the ninety-and-nine in their pasture. "Shepherd, the way is very rocky!" He does not seem to know what the way is, his heart is with his lost sheep. "Shepherd, it is a heavy climb up yon mountain side." He does not note his toil; his excitement lends him the feet of the wild goat; he stands securely where at other times his foot would slip. He looks around for his sheep and seems to see neither crag nor chasm. "Shepherd, it is a terrible path by which you must descend into yonder gloomy valley." It is not terrible to him: his only terror is lest his sheep should perish; he is taken up with that one fear, and nothing else. He leaps into danger, and escapes it by the one strong impulse which bears him on. It is grand to think of the Lord Jesus Christ with his heart set immovably upon the rescue of a soul which at this moment is lost to him.

It is *an active search* too; for observe, he goes after that which is lost, until he find it; and he does this with *a personal search.* He does not say to one of his underlings, "Here, hasten after that sheep which was lost, and bring it home." No, *he* follows it himself. And if ever there is a soul brought from sin to grace, it is not by us poor ministers working alone, but it is by the Master himself, who goes after his own sheep. It is glorious to think of him still personally tracking sinners, who, though they fly from him with a desperateness of folly, yet are still pursued by him—pursued by the Son of God, by the Eternal Lover of men—pursued by him until he finds them.

For notice *the perseverance of the search:* "until he find it." He does not stop till he has done the deed. You and I ought to seek after a soul, how long? Why, until we find it; for such is the model set before us by the Master. The parable says nothing about his not finding it; no hint of failure is given; we dream not that there may be a sheep belonging to him which he will never find. Oh, brethren, there are a great many whom you and I would never find; but when Jesus is after his own lost sheep, depend upon it such is his skill, so clearly doth he see, and so effectually doth he intervene, that he will surely bring them in. A defeated Christ I cannot conceive of. It is a personal search, and a persevering search, and *a successful search,* until he finds it. Let us praise and bless his name for this.

Observe that when the shepherd does find it, there is a little touch in the parable not often noticed,—he does not appear to put it back into the fold again: I mean, we do not find it so written, as a fact to be noted. I suppose he did so place it ultimately; but for the time being he keeps it with himself rather than with its fellows. The next scene is the shepherd at home, saying, "Rejoice with me; for I have found my sheep which was lost." It looks as if Jesus did not save a soul so much to the church as to himself, and though the saved are in the flock, the greatest joy of all is that the sheep is with the shepherd. This shows you how thoroughly Christ lays himself out that he may save his people. There is nothing in Christ that does not tend towards the salvation of his redeemed. There are no pull-backs with him, no half-consecrated influences which make him linger. In the pursuit of certain objects we lay out a portion of our faculties; but Jesus lays out all his powers upon the seeking and saving of souls.

The whole Christ seeks after each sinner; and when the Lord finds it, he gives himself to that one soul as if he had but that one soul to bless. How my heart admires the concentration of all the Godhead and manhood of Christ in his search after each sheep of his flock.

III. Now, we must pass on very briefly to notice a third point. We have had one subject of thought and one object of search; now we have ONE BURDEN OF LOVE. When the seeking is ended, then the saving appears,—"When he hath found it, he layeth it on his shoulders, rejoicing." Splendid action this! How beautifully the parable sets forth the whole of salvation. Some of the old writers delight to put it thus: in his incarnation he came after the lost sheep; in his life he continued to seek it; in his death he laid it upon his shoulders; in his resurrection he bore it on its way, and in his ascension he brought it home rejoicing. Our Lord's career is a course of soul-winning, a life laid out for his people; and in it you may trace the whole process of salvation.

But now, see, the shepherd finds the sheep, and he layeth it on his shoulders. It is *an uplifting action*, raising the fallen one from the earth whereon he hath strayed. It is as though he took the sheep just as it was, without a word of rebuke, without delay or hesitancy, and lifted it out of the slough or the briers into a place of safety. Do you not remember when the Lord lifted you up from the horrible pit? when he sent from above, and delivered you, and became your strength? I shall never forget that day. What a wonderful lift it was for me when the Great Shepherd lifted me into newness of life. The Lord said of Israel, "I bare you on eagles' wings;" but it is a dearer emblem still to be borne upon the shoulders of the incarnate Lord.

This laying on the shoulders was *an appropriating act.* He seemed to say, "You are my sheep, and therefore I lay you on my shoulders." He did not make his claim in so many words, but by a rapid action he declared it: for a man does not bear away a sheep to which he has no right: this was not a sheep-stealer, but a shepherd-proprietor. He holds fast the sheep by all four of its legs, so that it cannot stir, and then he lays it on his own shoulders, for it is all his own now. He seems to say, "I am a long way from home, and I am in a weary desert; but I have found my sheep, and these hands shall hold it." Here are our Lord's own words, "I give unto my sheep eternal life, and they shall never perish; neither shall any pluck them out of my hand." Hands of such might as those of Jesus will hold fast the found one. Shoulders of such power as those of Jesus will safely bear the found one home. It is all well with that sheep, for it is positively and experimentally the Good Shepherd's own, just as it always had been his in the eternal purpose of the Father. Do you remember when Jesus said unto you, "Thou art mine"? Then I know you also appropriated him, and began to sing—

"So I my best Beloved's am,
And he is mine."

More condescending still is another view of this act: it was *a deed of service* to the sheep. The sheep is uppermost, the weight of the sheep is upon the shepherd. The sheep rides, the shepherd is the burden-bearer. The sheep rests, the shepherd labours. "I am among you as he that serveth," said our Lord long ago. "Being found in fashion as a man, he humbled himself, and became obedient unto death, even the death of the cross." On that cross he bore the burden of our sin, and what is more, the burden of our very selves. Blessed be his name, "The Lord hath laid on him the iniquity of us all," and he hath laid us on him, too, and he beareth us. Remember that choice Scripture: "In his love and in his pity he redeemed them; and he bare them, and carried them all the days of old." Soul-melting thought, the Son of God became subservient to the sons of man! The Maker of heaven and earth bowed his shoulders to bear the weight of sinners.

It was a *rest-giving* act, very likely *needful* to the sheep which could go no further, and was faint and weary. It was a full rest to the poor creature if it could have understood it, to feel itself upon its shepherd's shoulders, irresistibly carried back to safety. What a rest it is to you and to me to know that we are borne along by the eternal power and Godhead of the Lord Jesus Christ! "The beloved of the Lord shall dwell in safety by him, and he shall dwell between his shoulders." The Christ upbears us to-day: we have no need of strength: our weakness is no impediment, for he bears us. Hath not the Lord said, "I have made, and I will bear; even I will carry and will deliver you"? We shall not even stumble, much less fall to ruin: the shepherd's feet shall traverse all the road in safety. No portion of the way back should cause us fear, for he is able to bear us even to his home above. What a sweet word is that in Deuteronomy: "The Lord thy God bare thee, as a man doth bear his son, in all the way that ye went, until ye came into this place." Blessed rest of faith, to give yourself up entirely to those hands and shoulders to keep and carry you even to the end! Let us bless and praise the Lord. The shepherd is consecrated to his burden: he bears nothing on his shoulders but his sheep; and the Lord Jesus seemeth to bear no burden but that of his people. He layeth out his omnipotence to save his chosen; having redeemed them first with price of blood, he redeems them still with all his power. "And they shall be mine, saith the Lord, in that day when I make up my jewels." Oh the glorious grace of our unfailing Saviour, who consecrates himself to our salvation, and concentrates upon that object all that he has and is!

IV. We close by noticing one more matter, which is—THE ONE SOURCE OF JOY. This man who had lost his sheep is filled with joy, but his sheep is the sole source of it. His sheep has so taken up all his thought, and so commanded all his faculties, that as he found all his care centred upon it, so he now finds all his joy flowing from it.

I invite you to notice the first mention of joy we get here: "When he hath found it, he layeth it on his shoulders, rejoicing." "That is a great load for you, shepherd!" Joyfully he answers, "I am glad to have it on my shoulders." The mother does not say when she has found her lost child, "This is a heavy load." No; she presses it to her bosom. She does not mind how heavy it is; it is a dear burden to her. She is rejoiced to bear it once again. "He layeth it on his shoulders, *rejoicing*." Remember that text: "Who for the joy that was set before him endured the cross, despising the shame." A great sorrow was on Christ when our load was laid on him; but a greater joy flashed into his mind when he thought that we were thus recovered from our lost estate. He said to himself, "I have taken them up upon my shoulders, and none can hurt them now, neither can they wander to destruction. I am bearing their sin, and they shall never come into condemnation. The penalty of their guilt has been laid n me that it may never be laid on them. I am an effectual and efficient Substitute for them. I am bearing, that they may never bear, my Father's righteous ire." His love to them made it a joy to feel every lash of the scourge of justice; his love to them made it a delight that the nails should pierce his hands and feet, and that his heart should be broken with the absence of his Father, God. Even "Eloi, Eloi, lama sabachthani," when the deeps of its woe have been sounded, will be found to have pearls of joy in its caverns. No shout of triumph can equal that cry of grief, because our Lord joyed to bear even the forsaking of his Father for the sin of his chosen whom he had loved from before the foundation of the world. Oh, you cannot understand it except in a very feeble measure! Let us try to find an earthly miniature likeness. A son is taken ill far away from home. He is laid sick with a fever, and a telegram is sent home. His mother says she *must* go and nurse him; she is wretched till she can set out upon the journey. It is a dreary place where her boy lies, but for the moment it is the dearest spot on earth to her. She joys to leave the comforts of her home to tarry among strangers for the love of her boy. She feels an intense joy in sacrificing herself; she refuses to retire from the bedside, she will not leave her charge; she watches day and night, and only from utter exhaustion does she fall asleep. You could not have kept her in England, she would have been too wretched. It was a great, deep, solemn pleasure for her to be where she could minister to her own beloved. Soul, remember you have given Jesus great joy in his saving you. He was for ever with the Father, eternally happy, infinitely glorious, as God over all; but yet he must needs come hither out of boundless love, take upon himself our nature, and suffer in our stead to bring us back to holiness and God. "He layeth it on his shoulders, rejoicing." That day the shepherd knew but one joy. He had found his sheep, and the very pressure of it upon his shoulders made his heart light, for he knew by that sign that the object of his care was safe beyond all question.

Now he goes home with it, and this joy of his was then so great that it filled his soul to overflowing. The parable speaks nothing as to his joy in getting home again, nor a word concerning the joy of being saluted by his friends and neighbours. No, the joy of having found his sheep eclipsed all other gladness of heart, and dimmed the light of home and friendship. He turns round to friends and neighbours and entreats them to help him to bear the weight of his happiness. He cries, "Rejoice with me, for I have found my sheep which was lost." One sinner had repented, and all heaven must make holiday concerning it. Oh, brethren, there is enough joy in the heart of Christ over his saved ones to flood all heaven with delight. The streets of Paradise run knee-deep with the heavenly waters of the Saviour's joy. They flow out of the very soul of Christ, and angels and glorified spirits bathe in the mighty stream. Let us do the same. We are friends if we are not neighbours. He calls us to-day to come and bring our hearts, like empty vessels, that he may fill them with his own joy, that our joy may be full. Those of us who are saved must enter into the joy of our Lord. When I was trying to think over this text I rejoiced with my Lord in the bringing in of each one of his sheep, for each one makes a heaven full of joy. But, oh to see all the redeemed brought in! Jesus would have no joy if he should lose one: it would seem to spoil it all. If the purpose of mercy were frustrated in any one instance it were a dreary defeat of the great Saviour. But his purpose shall be carried out in every instance. He "shall see of the travail of his soul, and shall be satisfied." He shall not fail nor be discouraged. He shall carry out the will of the Father. He shall have the full reward of his passion. Let us joy and rejoice with him this morning!

But the text tells us there was more joy over that one lost sheep than over the ninety-and-nine that went not astray. Who are these just persons that need no repentance? Well, you should never explain a parable so as to make it run on four legs if it was only meant to go on two. There may not be such persons at all, and yet the parable may be strictly accurate. If all of us had been such persons, and had never needed repentance, we should not have given as much joy to the heart of Christ as one sinner does when he repents. But suppose it to mean you and me who have long ago repented—who have, in a certain sense, now no need of repentance, because we are justified men and women—we do not give so much joy to the heart of God, for the time being, as a sinner does when he first returns unto God. It is not that it is a good thing to go astray, or a bad thing to be kept from it. You understand how that is: there are seven children in a family, and six of them are all well; but one dear child is taken seriously ill, and is brought near to the gates of death. It has recovered, its life is spared, and do you wonder that for the time being it gives more joy to the household than all the healthy ones? There is more expressed delight about it a great deal than over all those that have not been ill at all. This does not show it is a good thing to be ill. No, nothing of the kind; we are only speaking of *the joy* which comes of recovery from sickness. Take another case: you have a son who has been long away in a far country, and another son at home. You love them both equally, but when the absent son comes home he is for a season most upon your thoughts. Is it not natural that it should be so? Those at home give us joy constantly from day to day, but when the stream of joy has been dammed back by his absence, it pours down in a flood upon his return. Then we have "high days and holy days" and "bonfire nights."

There are special circumstances about repentance and conversion which produce joy over a restored wanderer. There was a preceding sorrow, and this sets off the joy by contrast. The shepherd was so touched with compassion for the lost sheep, that now his sorrow is inevitably turned into joy. He suffered a dreadful suspense, and that is a killing thing; it is like an acid eating into the soul. That suspense which makes one ask, Where is the sheep? Where can it be? is a piercing of the heart. All those weary hours of searching, and seeking, and following are painfully wearing to the heart. You feel as if you would almost sooner know that you never would find it than be in that doubtful state of mind. That suspense when it is ended naturally brings with it a sweet liberty of joy. Moreover, you know that the joy over penitents is so unselfish that you who have been kept by the grace of God for many years do not grieve that there should be more joy over a repenting sinner than over you. No, you say to yourself, "There is good cause. I am myself among those who are glad." You remember that good men made great rejoicing over you when you first came to Jesus; and you heartily unite with them in welcoming new-comers. You will not act the elder brother, and say I will not share the joy of my Father. Not a bit of it; but you will enter heartily into the music and dancing, and count it your heaven to see souls saved from hell. I feel a sudden flush and flood of delight when I meet with a poor creature who once lay at hell's dark door, but is now brought to the gate of heaven. Do not you?

The one thing I want to leave with you is how our gracious Lord seems to give himself up to his own redeemed. How entirely and perfectly every thought of his heart, every action of his power, goes toward the needy, guilty, lost soul. He spends his all to bring back his banished. Poor souls who believe in him have his whole strength engaged on their behalf. Blessed be his name! Now let all our hearts go forth in love towards him, who gave all his heart to work our redemption. Let us love him. We cannot love him as he loved us as to measure; but let us do so in like manner. Let us love him with all our heart and soul. Let us feel as if we saw nothing, knew nothing, loved nothing save Jesus crucified. As we filled all *his* heart let him fill all our hearts!

Oh, poor sinner, here to-day, will you not yield to the Good Shepherd? Will you not stand still as he draws near? Will you not submit to his mighty grace? Know that your rescue from sin and death must be of him, and of him alone. Breathe a prayer to him,—"Come, Lord, I wait for thy salvation! Save me, for I trust in thee." If thou dost thus pray, thou hast the mark upon thee of Christ's sheep, for he saith, "My sheep hear my voice, and I know them, and they follow me." Come to him, for he comes to you. Look to him for he looks to you.

Metropolitan Tabernacle Pulpit.

THE LOST SILVER PIECE.

A Sermon

DELIVERED ON LORD'S-DAY MORNING, JANUARY 15TH, 1871, BY

C. H. SPURGEON,

AT THE METROPOLITAN TABERNACLE, NEWINGTON.

"Either what woman having ten pieces of silver, if she lose one piece, doth not light a candle, and sweep the house, and seek diligently till she find it? And when she hath found it, she calleth her friends and her neighbours together, saying, Rejoice with me; for I have found the piece which I had lost. Likewise, I say unto you, there is joy in the presence of the angels of God over one sinner that repenteth."—Luke xv. 8—10.

THIS chapter is full of grace and truth. Its three consecutive parables have been thought to be merely a repetition of the same doctrine under different metaphors, and if that were so, the truth which it teaches is so important that it could not be rehearsed too often in our hearing. Moreover, it is one which we are apt to forget, and it is well to have it again and again impressed upon our minds. The truth here taught is just this—that mercy stretches forth her hand to misery, that grace receives men as sinners, that it deals with demerit, unworthiness, and worthlessness; that those who think themselves righteous are not the objects of divine compassion, but the unrighteous, the guilty, and the undeserving, are the proper subjects for the infinite mercy of God; in a word, that salvation is not of merit but of grace. This truth I say is most important, for it encourages penitents to return to their Father; but it is very apt to be forgotten, for even those who are saved by grace too often fall into the spirit of the elder brother, and speak as if, after all, their salvation depended on the works of the law.

But, my dear friends, the three parables recorded in this chapter are not repetitions; they all declare the same main truth, but each one reveals a different phase of it. The three parables are three sides of a vast pyramid of gospel doctrine, but there is a distinct inscription upon each. Not only in the similitude, but also in the teaching covered by the similitude, there is variety, progress, enlargement, discrimination. We have only need to read attentively to discover that in this trinity of parables, we have at once unity of essential truth and distinctness of description. Each one of the parables is needful to the other, and when combined they present us with a far more complete exposition of their doctrine than could have been conveyed by any one of them. Note for a moment the first of the three which brings before us a shepherd seeking a lost sheep. To whom does this refer? Who is the shepherd of Israel? Who brings again that which has gone astray? Do we not clearly discern the ever glorious and blessed Chief Shepherd of the sheep, who lays down his life that he may save them? Beyond a question, we see in the first parable the work of our Lord Jesus Christ. The second parable is most fitly placed where it is. It, I doubt not, represents the work of the Holy Spirit, working, through the church, for the lost but precious souls of men. The church is that woman who sweeps her house to find the lost piece of money, and in her the Spirit works his purposes of love. Now the work of the Holy Spirit follows the work of Christ. As here we first see the shepherd seeking the lost sheep, and then read of the woman seeking the lost piece of money, so the great Shepherd redeems, and then the Holy Spirit restores the soul. You will perceive that each parable is thoroughly understood in its minute details when so interpreted. The shepherd seeks a sheep which has wilfully gone astray, and so far the element of sin is present; the lost piece of money does not bring up that idea, nor was it needful that it should, since the parable does not deal with the pardon of sin as the first does. The sheep, on the other hand, though stupid is not altogether senseless and dead, but the piece of money is altogether unconscious and powerless, and therefore all the fitter emblem of man as the Holy Ghost begins to deal with him, dead in trespasses and sins. The third parable evidently represents the divine Father in his abundant love receiving the lost child who comes back to him. The third parable would be likely to be misunderstood without the first and the second. We have sometimes heard it said—here is the prodigal received as soon as he comes back, no mention being made of a Saviour who seeks and saves him. Is it possible to teach all truths in one single parable? Does not the first one speak of the shepherd seeking the lost sheep? Why need repeat what had been said before? It has also been said that the prodigal returned of his own free will, for there is no hint of the operation of a superior power upon his heart, it seems as if he himself spontaneously says, "I will arise, and go unto my Father." The answer is, that the Holy Spirit's work had been clearly described in the second parable, and needed not to be introduced again. If you put the three pictures in a line, they represent the whole compass of salvation, but each one apart sets forth the work in reference to one or other of the divine persons of the blessed Trinity. The shepherd, with much pain and self-sacrifice, seeks the reckless, wandering sheep; the woman diligently searches for the insensible but lost piece of money; the father receives the returning prodigal. What God has joined together, let no man put asunder. The three life-sketches are one, and one truth is taught in the whole three, yet each one is distinct from the other, and by itself instructive.

May we be taught of God while we try to discover the mind of the Spirit in this parable, which, as we believe, represents the work of the Holy Spirit in and through the church. The church is evermore represented as a woman, either the chaste bride of Christ, or the shameless courtesan of Babylon; as for good a woman sweeps the house, so for evil a woman takes the leaven and hides it in the meal till all is leavened. Towards Christ a wife and towards men a mother, the church is most fitly set forth as a woman. A woman with a house under her control is the full idea of the text, her husband away and herself in charge of the treasure: just such is the condition of the church since the departure of the Lord Jesus to the Father.

To bring each part of the text under inspection we shall notice man in three conditions—*lost, sought, found.*

I. First, the parable treats of man, the object of divine mercy, as LOST.

Notice, first, the treasure was *lost in the dust.* The woman had lost her piece of silver, and in order to find it she had to sweep for it, which proves that it had fallen into a dusty place, fallen to the earth, where it might be hidden and concealed amid rubbish and dirt. Every man of Adam born is as a piece of silver lost, fallen, dishonoured, and some are buried amid foulness and dust. If we should drop many pieces of money they would fall into different positions; one of them might fall into actual mire, and be lost there; another might fall upon a carpet, a cloth, or a clean, well-polished floor, and be lost there. If you have lost your money, it is equally lost into whatever place it may have fallen. So all men are alike lost, but they have not all fallen into the like condition of apparent defilement. One man from the surroundings of his childhood and the influences of education, has never indulged in the coarser and more brutalising vices; he has never been a blasphemer, perhaps never openly even a Sabbath-breaker, yet he may be lost for all that. Another, on the other hand, has fallen into great excess of riot; he is familiar with wantonness and chambering, and all manner of evil; he is lost, he is lost with an emphasis: but the more decorous sinner is lost also. There may be some here this morning (and we wish always to apply the truth as we go on), who are lost in the very worst of corruption: I would to God that they would take hope and learn from the parable before us, that the church of God and the Spirit of God are seeking after them, and they may be among the found ones yet. Since, on the other hand, there are many here who have not dropped into such unclean places, I would affectionately remind them that they are nevertheless lost, and they need as much to be sought for by the Spirit of God as if they were among the vilest of the vile. To save the moral needs divine grace as certainly as to save the immoral. If you be lost, my dear hearer, it will be small avail to you that you perished respectably, and were accursed in decent company: if you lack but one thing, yet if the deficiency be fatal, it will be but a poor consolation that you had only one lack. If one leak sent the vessel to the bottom; it was no comfort to the crew that their ship only leaked in one place. One disease may kill a man; he may be sound everywhere else, but it will be a sorry comfort to him to know that he might have lived long had but that one organ been sound. If, dear hearer, thou shouldst have no sin whatever save only an evil heart of unbelief, if all thy external life should be lovely and amiable, yet if that one fatal sin be in thee, thou canst draw small consolation from all else that is good about thee. Thou art lost by nature, and thou must be found by grace, whoever thou mayst be.

In this parable that which was lost was *altogether ignorant of its being lost.* The silver coin was not a living thing, and therefore had no consciousness of its being lost or sought after. The piece of money lost was quite as content to be on the floor or in the dust, as it was to be in the purse of its owner amongst its like. It knew nothing about its being lost, and could not know. And it is just so with the sinner who is spiritually dead in sin, he is unconscious of his state, nor can we make him understand the danger and terror of his condition. When he feels that he is lost, there is already some work of grace in him. When the sinner knows that he is lost, he is no longer content with his condition, but begins to cry out for mercy, which is evidence that the finding work has already begun. The unconverted sinner will confess that he is lost because he knows the statement to be scriptural, and therefore out of compliment to God's word he admits it to be true, but he has no idea of what is meant by it, else would he either deny it with proud indignation, or he would bestir himself to pray that he might be restored to the place from which he has fallen, and be numbered with Christ's precious property. O my hearers, this it is that makes the Spirit of God so needful in all our preachings, and every other soul-saving exercise, because we have to deal with insensible souls. The man who puts the fire-escape against the window of a burning house, may readily enough rescue those who are aware of their danger, and who rush to the front and help him, or at least are submissive to him in his work of delivering them; but if a man were insane, if he played with the flames, if he were idiotic and thought that some grand illumination were going on, and knew nothing of the danger but was only "glamoured by the glare," then would it be hard work for the rescuer. Even thus it is with sinners. They know not, though they profess to know, that sin is hell, that to be an alien from God is to be condemned already, to live in sin is to be dead while you live. The insensibility of the piece of money fairly pictures the utter indifference of souls unquickened by divine grace.

The silver piece was *lost but not forgotten.* The woman knew that she had ten pieces of silver originally; she counted them over carefully, for they were all her little store, and she found only nine, but she well remembered that one more was hers and ought to be in her hand. This is our hope for the Lord's lost ones, they are lost but not forgotten, the heart of the Saviour remembers them, and prays for them. O soul, I trust you are one whom Jesus calls his own, if so he remembers the pangs which he endured in redeeming you, and he recollects the Father's love which was reflected on you from old eternity, when the Father gave you into the hands of his beloved Son. You are not forgotten of the Holy Spirit who seeks you for the Saviour. This is the minister's hope, that there is a people whom the Lord remembers and whom he never will forget, though they forget him Strangers to him, far-off, ignorant, callous, careless, dead, yet the everlasting heart in heaven throbs towards them with love; and the mind of the Spirit, working on earth, is directed to them. These, who were numbered and reckoned up of old are still in the inventory of the divine memory; and though lost they are earnestly remembered still. In some sense this is true of every sinner here. You are lost, but that you are remembered is evident, for I am sent to-day to preach the gospel of Jesus to you. God has thoughts of love concerning you, and bids you turn unto him and live. Have respect, I pray you, to the word of his salvation.

Next, the piece of silver was *lost but still claimed.* Observe that the woman called the money, "*my* piece which was lost." When she lost its possession she did not lose her right to it; it did not become somebody else's when it slipped out of her hand and fell upon the floor. Those for whom Christ hath died, whom he hath peculiarly redeemed, are not Satan's even when they are dead in sin. They may come under the devil's usurped dominion, but the monster shall be chased from his throne. Christ has received them of old of the Father, and he has bought them with his precious blood, and he will have them; he will chase away the intruder and claim his own. Thus saith the Lord, "Your covenant with death is disannulled, and your agreement with hell shall not stand." Ye have sold yourselves for nought; and ye shall be redeemed without money. Jesus shall have his own, and none shall pluck them from his hold; he will defend his claim against all comers.

Further, observe that the lost piece of money was not only remembered and claimed, but *it was also valued.* In these three parables the value of the lost article steadily rises. This is not very clear at first sight, because it may be said that a sheep is of more value than a piece of money; but notice that the shepherd only lost one sheep out of a hundred, but the woman lost one piece out of ten, and the father one son out of two. Now, it is not the value of the thing in itself which is here set forth, for the soul of a man, as absolutely valued in comparison with the infinite God, is of small esteem; but because of his love it is of great value to him. The one piece of money to the woman was a tenth part of all she had, and it was very valuable in her esteem. To the Lord of love a lost soul is very precious: it is not because of its intrinsic value, but it has a relative value which God sets at a high rate. The Holy Spirit values souls, and therefore the church prizes them too. The church sometimes says to herself, "We have but few conversions, few members; many are called, but few chosen." She counts over her few converts, her few members, and one soul is to her all the more precious because of the few there are who in these times are in the treasury of Christ, stamped with the image of the great King, and made of the precious genuine silver of God's own grace. O dear friend, you think yourself of small value, you who are conscious that you have sinned, but the church does not think you of small value, and the Holy Spirit does not despise you. He sets a high price upon you, and so do his people. We value your souls, we only wish we knew how to save them; we would spare no expense or pains if we might but be the means of finding you, and bringing you once more into the great Owner's hand.

The piece of money was lost, but *it was not lost hopelessly.* The woman had hopes of recovering it, and therefore she did not despair, but set to work at once. It is a dreadful thing to think of those souls which are lost hopelessly. Their state reminds me of a paragraph I have cut from this week's newspaper:—"The fishing smack Veto of Grimsby, S. Cousins, master, arrived in port from the Dogger Bank on Saturday night. The master reports that on the previous Wednesday, when about two hundred miles from Spurn, he sighted to the leeward what at first appeared to be a small schooner in distress, but on bearing down to her found her to be a full-sized lifeboat, upwards of twenty feet long, and full of water up to her corks. There was no name on the boat, which had evidently belonged to some large ship or steamer. It was painted white both inside and out, with a brown streak round the rim. When alongside, on closer examination, three dead sailors were perceived lying aft, huddled together, and a fourth athwart in the bow, with his head hanging over the rowlocks. They seemed from their dress and general appearance to be foreigners, but the bodies had been frightfully 'washed about,' and were in a state of decomposition, and had evidently been dead some weeks. The water-logged waif drifted on with its ghastly cargo, and the horrible sight so shocked the crew of the Veto that afterwards they were almost too unnerved to attend to their trawling, and the smack, in consequence, returned to port with a comparatively small catch, and sooner than expected." Do you wonder at the men sickening in the presence of this mystery of the sea? I shudder as I think I see that Charon-like boat floating on and on; mercy need not follow it, she can confer no boon; love need not seek it, no deed of hers can save. My soul sees, as in a vision, souls hopelessly lost, drifting on the waves of eternity, beyond all hope or help. Alas! Alas! Millions of our race are now in that condition. Upon them has passed the second death, and powerless are we all to save them. Towards them even the gospel has no aspect of hope. Our joy is that we have to deal to-day with lost souls who are not yet hopelessly lost. They are dead in sin, but there is a quickening power which can make them live. O mariner of the sea of life, fisher of men upon this stormy sea, those castaways whom you meet with are accessible to your efforts of compassion, they can be rescued from the pitiless deeps; your mission is not a hopeless one. I rejoice over the ungodly man here to-day that he is not in torment, not in hell, he is not among those whose worm dieth not and whose fire is not quenched. I congratulate the Christian church too, that her piece of money has not fallen where she cannot find it. I rejoice that the fallen around us are not past hope; yea, though they dwell in the worst dens of London, though they be thieves and harlots, they are not beyond the reach of mercy. Up, O church of God, while possibilities of mercy remain! Gird up your loins, ye soul-winners, and resolve by the grace of God that every hour of hope shall be well employed by you.

One other point is worthy of notice. The piece of silver was lost, but it was *lost in the house*, and the woman knew it to be so. If she had lost it in the streets, the probabilities are she would not have looked for it again, for other hands might have closed over it. If she had lost it in a river, or dropped it in the sea, she might very fairly have concluded that it was gone for ever, but evidently she was sure that she had lost it in the house. Is it not a consolation to know that those here, who are lost, are still in the house? They are still under the means of grace, within the sphere of the church's operations, within the habitation of which she is the mistress, and where the Holy Spirit works. What thankfulness there ought to be in your minds that you are not lost as heathens, nor lost amid Romish or Mohammedan superstition, but lost where the gospel is faithfully and plainly preached to you; where you are lovingly told, that whosoever believeth in Christ

Jesus is not condemned. Lost, but lost where the church's business is to look after you, where it is the Spirit's work to seek and to find you.

This is the condition of the lost soul, depicted as a lost piece of silver

II. Secondly, we shall notice the soul under another condition, we shall view it as SOUGHT.

By whom was the piece of silver sought? It was *sought by its owner personally.* Notice, she who lost the money lit a candle and swept the house, and sought diligently till *she* found it. So, brethren, I have said that the woman represents the Holy Spirit, or rather the church in which the Holy Spirit dwells. Now, there will never be a soul found till the Holy Spirit seeks after it. He is the great soul finder. The heart will continue in the dark until he comes with his illuminating power. He is the owner, he possesses it, and he alone can effectually seek after it. The God to whom the soul belongs must seek the soul. But he does it by his church, for souls belong to the church too; they are sons and daughters of the chosen mother, they are her citizens and treasures. For this reason the church must personally seek after souls. She cannot delegate her work to anybody. The woman did not pay a servant to sweep the house, but she swept it herself. Her eyes were much better than a servant's eyes, for the servant's eyes would only look after somebody else's money, and perhaps would not see it; but the mistress would look after her own money, and she would be certain to light upon it if it were anywhere within sight. When the church of God solemnly feels, "It is our work to look after sinners, we must not delegate it even to the minister, or to the City-missionary, or the Bible-woman, but the church as a church must look after the souls of sinners," then I believe souls will be found and saved. When the church recognises that these lost souls belong to her, she will be likely to find them. It will be a happy day when every church of God is actively at work for the salvation of sinners. It has been the curse of Christendom that she has ventured to delegate her sacred duties to men called priests, or that she has set apart certain persons to be called *the religious*, who are to do works of mercy and charity and of evangelisation. We are, every one of us who are Christ's, bound to do our own share; nay, we should deem it a privilege of which we will not be deprived, personally to serve God, personally to sweep the house and search after the lost spiritual treasures. The church herself, in the power of the indwelling Spirit of God, must seek lost souls.

Note that this seeking became *a matter of chief concern* with the woman. I do not know what other business she had to do, but I do know that she put it all by to find the piece of money. There was the corn to be ground for the morning meal, perhaps that was done, at any rate, if not so, she left it unprepared. There was a garment to be mended, or water to be drawn, or the fire to be kindled, or the friends and neighbours to be conversed with—never mind, the mistress forgets everything else, she has lost her piece of money, and she must find it at once. So with the church of God, her chief concern should be to seek the perishing sons of men. To bring souls to know Jesus, and to be saved in him with a great salvation should be the church's great longing and concern. She has other things to do. She has her own edification to consider, she has other matters to be attended to in their place, but this first, this evermore and always first. The woman evidently said, "The money is lost, I must find that first." The loss of her piece of silver was so serious a matter that if she sat down to her mending, her hands would miss their nimbleness, or if any other household work demanded her attention, it would be an irksome task to her, for she was thinking of that piece of coin. If her friend came and talked with her, she would say to herself, "I wish she were gone, for I want to be looking after my lost money." I wish the church of God had such an engrossing love for poor sinners that she would feel everything to be an impertinence which hindered her from soul-saving. We have every now and then, as a church, a little to do with politics, and a little to do with finance, for we are still in the world, but I love to see in all churches everything kept in the background, compared with soul-saving work. This must be first and foremost. Educate the people—yes, certainly; we take an interest in everything which will do good to our fellow citizens, for we are men as well as Christians; but first and foremost our business is to win souls, to bring men to Jesus, to hunt up those who bear heaven's image, though lost and fallen. This is what we must be devoted to, this is the main and chief concern of believers, the very reason for the existence of a church; if she regard it not, she forgets her highest end.

Now note, that the woman having thus set her heart to find her money, *she used the most fit and proper means* to accomplish her end. First, she lit a candle. So doth the Holy Spirit in the church. In Eastern dwellings it would be necessary, if you lost a piece of money and wanted to find it, to light a candle at any time; for in our Saviour's day glass was not used, and the windows of houses were only little slits in the side of the wall, and the rooms were very dark. Almost all the Oriental houses are very dark to this day, and if anything be dropped as small as a piece of silver, it must be looked for with a candle even at high noon. Now, the sphere in which the church moves here on earth is a dim twilight of mental ignorance, and moral darkness, and in order to find a lost soul, light must be brought to bear upon it. The Holy Spirit uses the light of the gospel; he convinces men of sin, of righteousness, and of judgment to come. The woman lit a candle, and even thus the Holy Spirit lights up some chosen man whom he makes to be a light in the world. He calls to himself whomsoever he wills, and makes him a lamp to shine upon the people. Such a man will have to be consumed in his calling, like a candle he will be burnt up in light-giving. Earnest zeal, and laborious self-sacrifice, will eat him up. So may this church, and every church of God, be continually using up her anointed men and women, who shall be as lights in the midst of a crooked and perverse generation, to find out lost souls.

But she was not content with her candle, she fetched her broom, she swept the house. If she could not find the silver as things were in the house, she brought the broom to bear upon the accumulated dust. Oh, how a Christian church, when it is moved by the Holy Spirit, cleanses herself and purges all her work! "Perhaps," saith she, "some of our members are inconsistent, and so men are hardened in sin; these offenders must be put away. The tone of religion is low—that may be hindering the conversion of souls, it must be raised. Perhaps our statements of truth, and our ways of proclaiming it, are not the most likely to command attention, we must amend them; we must use the best possible methods, we must in fact sweep the whole house." I delight to see an earnest house-sweeping by confession of sin at a prayer meeting, or by a searching discourse, a house-sweeping when every one is earnest to reform himself, and to get nearer to God himself by a revival of his own personal piety. This is one of the means by which the church is enabled to find the hidden ones. Besides this, all the neighbourhood round the church (for the house is the sphere in which the church moves), must be ransacked, stirred, turned over, in a word "swept." A church that is really in earnest after souls will endeavour to penetrate the gloom of poverty and stir the heaps of profligacy. She will hunt high and hunt low if by any means she may rescue from destruction the precious thing upon which her heart is set.

Carefully note that this seeking after the lost piece of silver with fitting instruments, the broom and the candle, was *attended with no small stir.* She swept the house—there was dust for her eyes; if any neighbours were in the house there was dust for them. You cannot sweep a house without causing some confusion and temporary discomfort. We sometimes hear persons complain of certain Christians for making too much ado about religion. The complaint shows that something is being done, and in all probability some success being achieved. Those people who have no interest in the lost silver are annoyed at the dust; it is getting down their throats, and they cough at it; never mind, good woman, sweep again, and make them grumble more. Another will say, "I do not approve of religious excitement, I am for quiet and orderly modes of procedure." I dare say that this good woman's neighbour, when she came in to make a call, exclaimed in disgust, "Why, mistress, there is not a chair to sit down upon in comfort, and you are so taken up about this lost money that you scarce give me an answer. Why, you are wasting candle at a great rate, and seem quite in a fever." "Well," the good woman would answer, "but I must find my piece of silver, and in order to seek it out I can bear a little dust myself, and so must you if you wish to stop here while I am searching." An earnest church will be sure to experience a degree of excitement when it is soul-hunting, and very cautious, very fastidious, very critical people will find fault. Never mind them, my brethren, sweep on and let them talk on. Never mind making a dust if you find the money. If souls be saved irregularities and singularities are as the small dust of the balance. If men be brought to Jesus, care nothing what cavillers say. Sweep on, sweep on, even though men exclaim, "They that turn the world upside down are come hither also." Though confusion and stir, and even persecution be the present result, yet if the finding of an immortal soul be the ultimate effect, you will be well repaid for it.

It is to be remarked, also, that in the seeking of this piece of silver the coin was *sought in a most engrossing manner.* For a time nothing was thought of but the lost silver. Here is a candle: the good woman does not read by the light of it, nor mend her garments; no, but the candle-light is all spent on that piece of money. All its light is consecrated to the search. Here is a broom: there is other work for the broom to do, but for the present it sweeps for the silver and for nothing else. Here are two bright eyes in the good woman's head: ay, but they look for nothing but the lost money; she does not care what else may be in the house or out of it—her money she cares for, and that she must find; and here she is with candle, broom, strength, eyesight, faculties of mind, and limbs of body, all employed in searching for the lost treasure. It is just so when the Holy Ghost works in a church, the preacher, like a candle, yields his light, but it is all with the view of finding out the sinner and letting him see his lost estate. Whether it be the broom of the law or the light of the gospel, all is meant for the sinner. All the Holy Spirit's wisdom is engaged to find the sinner, and all the living church's talent and substance and power are put forth if by any means the sinner may be saved. It is a fair picture, may I see it daily. How earnestly souls are sought for when the Spirit of God is truly in his church!

One other thought only. This woman *sought for her piece of silver continuously*—"till she found it." May you and I, as parts of the church of God, look after wandering souls till we find them. We say they discourage us. No doubt that piece of silver did discourage the woman who sought it. We complain that men do not appear inclined to religion. Did the piece of money lend the housewife any help? Was it any assistance to her? She did the seeking, she did it all. And the Holy Ghost through you, my brother, seeks the salvation of the sinner, not expecting the sinner to help him, for the sinner is averse to being found. What, were you repulsed the other day by one whose spiritual good you longed for? Go again! Where your invitations laughed at? Invite again! Did you become the subject of ridicule through your earnest entreaties? Entreat again! Those are not always the least likely to be saved who at first repel our efforts. A harsh reception is sometimes only an intimation that the heart recognises the power of the truth, though it does not desire at present to yield to it. Persevere, brother, till you find the soul you seek. You who spend so much effort in your Sunday-school class, use still your candle, enlighten the child's mind still, sweep the house till you find what you seek; never give up the child till it is brought to Christ. You, in your senior class, dealing with that young man or young woman, cease not from your private prayers and from your personal admonitions, till that heart belongs to Jesus. You who can preach in the streets, or visit the lodging-houses, or go from door to door with tracts, I charge you all, for you can all do something, never give up the pursuit of sinners until they are safely lodged in Jesus' hands. We must have them saved! With all the intense perseverance of the woman who turned everything upside down, and counted all things but loss that she might but find her treasure, so may we also, the Spirit of God working in us, upset everything of rule and conventionality, and form and difficulty, if we may but by any means save some, and bring out of the dust those who bear the King's image, and are dear to the King's heart.

III. Time has fled, alas! too swiftly, and so I must close with the third point, which is the piece of silver FOUND.

Found! In the first place, this was *the woman's ultimatum, and nothing short of it.* She never stopped until the coin was found. So it is the Holy Spirit's design, not that the sinner should be brought into a hopeful state, but that he should be actually saved: and this is the church's great concern, not that people be made hearers, not that they be made orthodox professors, but that they be really changed and renewed, regenerated and born again.

The woman herself found the piece of money. It did not turn up by accident, nor did some neighbour step in and find it. The Spirit of God himself finds sinners, and the church of God herself as a rule is the instrument of their recovery. Dear brethren, a few years ago there was a kind of slur cast upon the visible church, by many enthusiastic but mistaken persons, who dreamed that the time was come for doing away with organised effort, for irregular agencies outside of the visible church were to do all the work. Certain remarkable men sprang up whose ferocious censures almost amounted to attacks upon the recognised churches. Their efforts were apart from the regular ministry, and in some cases ostentatiously in opposition to it. It was as much their aim to pull down the existing church as to bring in converts. I ask any man who has fairly watched these efforts, what they have come to? I never condemned them, nor will I; but I do venture to say to-day in the light of their history, that they have not superseded regular church work and never will. The masses were to be aroused, but where are the boasted results? What has become of many of these much-vaunted works? Those who have worked in connection with a church of God have achieved permanent usefulness; those who acted as separatist agencies, though they blazed for awhile before the public eye and filled the corners of the newspapers with spiritual puffery, are now either altogether or almost extinct. Where are the victories which were to be won by these free-shooters? Echo answers, Where? We have to fall back on the old disciplined troops. God means to bless the church still, and it is through the church that he will continue to send a benediction upon the sons of men. I am glad to hear of anybody preaching the gospel; if Christ is preached I therein do rejoice, yea, and will rejoice. I remember the Master's words, "Forbid them not! He that is not against us is for us." Still the mass of conversions will come through the church, and by her regular organised efforts. The woman who lights the candle and sweeps the house, to whom the silver belongs, will herself find it.

Now notice when she had found it what she did, *she rejoiced.* The greater her trouble in searching, the higher her joy in finding. What joy there is in the church of God when sinners are converted! We have our high holidays, we have our mirthful days downstairs in the lecture hall, when we hear of souls turned from the paths of the destroyer; and in the vestries behind, your pastors and elders often experience such joy as only heaven can equal, when we have heard the stories of souls emancipated from the slavery of sin, and led into the perfect liberty which Jesus gives. The church rejoices.

Next, she *calls her friends and neighbours* to share her joy. I am afraid we do not treat our friends and neighbours with quite enough respect, or remember to invite them to our joys. Who are they? I think the angels are here meant; not only the angels in heaven, but those who are watching here below. Note well, that when the shepherd took home the sheep, it is written, "There *shall be* joy *in heaven* over one sinner that repenteth ;" but it does not mention heaven here, nor speak of the future, but it is written, "*There is* joy in the presence of the angels of God." Now, the church is on earth, and the Holy Spirit is on earth, at work ; when there is a soul saved, the angels down below, who keep watch and ward around the faithful, and so are our friends and neighbours, rejoice with us. Know ye not that angels are present in our assemblies? for this reason the apostle tells us that the woman hath her head covered in the assembly. He saith, "Because of the angels, for they love order and decorum." The angels are wherever the saints are, beholding our orders and rejoicing in our joy. When we see conversions we may bid them rejoice too, and they will praise God with us. I do not suppose the rejoicing ends there; for as angels are always ascending and descending upon the Son of Man, they soon convey the tidings to the hosts above, and heaven rejoices over one repenting sinner.

The joy is a present joy; it is a joy in the house, in the church in her own sphere ; it is the joy of her neighbours who are round about her here below. All other joy seems swallowed up in this: as every other occupation was suspended to find the lost silver, so every other joy is hushed when the precious thing is found. The church of God has a thousand joys—the joy of her saints ascending to the skies, the joy of her saints ripening for glory, the joy of such as contend with sin and overcome it, and grow in grace and receive the promise; but the chief joy in the church, which swallows all others, as Aaron's rod swallowed up the other rods, is the joy over the lost soul which, after much sweeping and searching, is found at last.

The practical lesson to the unconverted is just this. Dear friend, *see what value is set upon you.* You think that nobody cares for you—why, heaven and earth care for you! You say, "I am as nothing, a castaway, and I am utterly worthless." No, you are not worthless to the blessed Spirit, nor worthless to the church of God—she longs for you.

See, again, *how false that suspicion of yours is that you will not be welcome* if you come to Christ. Welcome! welcome! why, the church is searching for you; the Spirit of God is searching for you. Do not talk of welcome, you will be a great deal more than welcome. Oh, how glad will Christ be, and the Spirit be, and the church be, to receive you! Ah! but you complain that you have done nothing to make you fit for mercy. Talk not so, what had the lost piece of money done? What could it do? It was lost and helpless. They who sought it did all; he who seeks you will do all for you. O poor soul, since Christ now bids thee come, come! If his Spirit draws thee, yield! Since the promise now speaks, "Come now, and let us reason together: though your sins be as scarlet, they shall be as white as snow; though they be red like crimson, they shall be as wool," accept the promise. Believe in Jesus. God bless you and save you, for Jesus' sake. Amen.

PORTIONS OF SCRIPTURE READ BEFORE SERMON—Psalm cxxxvi. and Luke xv.

The New Park Street Pulpit.

THE SYMPATHY OF THE TWO WORLDS.

A Sermon

DELIVERED ON SABBATH MORNING, JULY 4, 1858, BY THE

REV. C. H. SPURGEON,

AT THE MUSIC HALL, ROYAL SURREY GARDENS.

"There is joy in the presence of the angels of God over one sinner that repenteth."—Luke xv. 10.

MAN'S heart is never big enough to hold either its joys or its sorrows. You never heard of a man whose heart was exactly full of sorrow; for no sooner is it full, than it overflows. The first prompting of the soul is to tell its sorrow to another. The reason is, that our heart is not large enough to hold our grief; and we need to have another heart to receive a portion thereof. It is even so with our joy. When the heart is full of joy, it always allows its joy to escape. It is like the fountain in the market-place; whenever it is full it runs away in streams, and so soon as it ceases to overflow, you may be quite sure that it has ceased to be full. The only full heart is the overflowing heart. You know this, beloved, you have proved it to be true; for when your soul has been full of joy, you have first called together your own kindred and friends, and you have communicated to them the cause of your gladness; and when those vessels have been full even to the brim, you have been like the woman who borrowed empty vessels of her neighbours, for you have asked each of them to become partakers in your joy, and when the hearts of all your neighbours have been full, you have felt as if they were not large enough, and the whole world has been called upon to join in your praise. You bade the fathomless ocean drink in your joy; you spoke to the trees and bade them clap their hands, while the mountains and hills were invoked by you to break forth into singing; the very stars of heaven seemed to look down upon you, and you bade them sing for you, and all the world was full of music through the music that was in your heart. And, after all, what is man but the great musician of the world? The universe is a great organ with mighty pipes. Space, time, eternity, are like the throats of this great organ; and man, a little creature, puts his fingers on the keys, and wakes the universe to thunders of harmony, stirring up the whole creation to mightiest acclamations of praise. Know ye not that man is God's high priest in the universe? All things else are but the sacrifice; but he is the priest,—carrying in his heart the fire, and in his hand the wood, and in his mouth the two-edged sword of dedication, with which he offers up all things to God.

But I have no doubt, beloved, the thought has sometimes struck us that our praise does not go far enough. We seem as if we dwelt in an isle cut off from the mainland. This world, like a fair planet, swims in a sea of ether unnavigated by mortal ship. We have sometimes thought that surely our praise was confined to the shores of this poor narrow world, that it was impossible for us to pull the ropes which might ring the bells of heaven, that we could by no means whatever reach our hands so high as to sweep the celestial chords of angelic harps. We have said to ourselves there is no connection between earth and heaven. A huge black wall divides us. A strait of unnavigable waters shuts us out. Our prayers cannot reach to heaven, neither can our praises affect the celestials. Let us learn from our text how mistaken we are. We are, after all, however much we seem to be shut out from heaven, and from the great universe, but a province of God's vast united empire, and what is done on earth is known in heaven; what is sung on earth is sung in heaven; and there is a sense in which it is true that the tears of earth are wept again in paradise, and the sorrows of mankind are felt again, even on the throne of the Most High.

My text tells us, "There is joy in the presence of the angels of God, over one sinner that repenteth." It seems as if it showed me a bridge by which I might cross over into eternity. It doth, as it were, exhibit to me, certain magnetic wires which convey the intelligence of what is done here to spirits in another world. It teaches me that there is a real and wonderful connection between this lower world, and that which is beyond the skies, where God dwelleth, in the land ot the happy.

We shall talk about that subject a little this morning. My first head will be *the sympathy of the world above with the world below*; the second, *the judgment of the angels*,—they rejoice over repenting sinners; we shall see what is their ground for so doing. The third, will be *a lesson for the saints*; if the angels in heaven rejoice over repenting sinners, so should we.

I. In the first place, our text teaches us THE SYMPATHY OF THE TWO WORLDS. Imagine not, O son of man, that thou art cut off from heaven: for there is a ladder, the top whereof doth rest at the foot of the throne of the Almighty, the base whereof is fixed in the lowest place of man's misery! Conceive not that there is a great gulph fixed between thee and the *Father*, across which his mercy cannot come, and over which thy prayers and faith can never leap. Oh, think not, son of man, that thou dwellest in a storm-girt island, cut off from the continent of eternity. I beseech thee, believe that there is a bridge across that chasm, a road along which feet may travel. This world is not separated, for all creation is but one body. And know thou, O son of man, though thou in this world doth but dwell, as it were on the foot, yet from the feet even to the head, there are nerves and veins that do unite the whole. The same great heart which beats in heaven beats on earth. The love of the *Eternal Father* which cheers the celestial, makes glad the terrestrial too. Rest assured that though the glory of the celestial be one and the glory of the terrestrial be another, yet are they but another in appearance, for after all, they are the same. Oh! list thee, son of man, and thou wilt soon learn that thou art no stranger in a strange land—a houseless Joseph in the land of Egypt, shut out from his Father, and his children, who still remain in the happy paradise of Canaan. No, thy Father loves thee still. There is a connection between thee and him. Strange that though leagues of distance lie between the finite creature and the infinite Creator, yet there are links that unite us both! When a tear is wept by thee, think not thy Father doth not behold; for, "Like as a father pitieth his children so the Lord pitieth them that fear him." Thy sigh is able to move the heart of Jehovah; thy whisper can incline his ear unto thee; thy prayer can stay his hands; thy faith can move his arm. Oh! think not that God sits on high in an eternal slumber, taking no account of thee. "Shall a mother forget her suckling child, that she should not have compassion on the son of her womb? Yea, she may forget, yet will I not forget thee." Engraven upon the Father's hand thy name remains; and on his heart recorded there thy person stands. He thought of thee before the worlds were made; before the channels of the sea were scooped, or the gigantic mountains lifted their heads in the white clouds, he thought of thee. He thinketh on thee still. "I, the Lord, do keep it; I will water it every moment: lest any hurt it, I will keep it night and day." For the eyes of the Lord run to and fro in every place, to show himself strong on the behalf of all them that fear him. Thou art not cut off from him. Thou dost move in him; in him thou dost live and have thy being. "He is a very present help in time of trouble."

Remember, again, O heir of immortality, that thou art not only linked to the Godhead, but th ere is another one in heaven with whom thou hast a strange, yet near connection. In the centre of the throne sits one who is thy brother, allied to thee by blood. *The Son of God,* eternal, equal with his Father, became in the fulness of time the Son of Mary, an infant of a span long. He was, yea is, bone of thy bone and flesh of thy flesh. Think not that thou art cut off from the celestial world, while he is there; for is he not thy head, and hath he not himself declared that thou art a member of his body, of his flesh and of his bones? Oh, man, thou art not separated from heaven whilst Jesus tells thee—

"I feel at my heart all thy sighs and thy groans,
For thou art most near me, my flesh and my bones,
In all thy distresses, thy Head feels the pain,
They all are most needful, not one is in vain."

Oh, poor, disconsolate mourner, Christ remembers thee every hour. Thy sighs are his sighs; thy groans are his groans; thy prayers are his prayers:—

"He in his measure feels afresh,
What every member bears."

Crucified he is when thou art crucified; he dies when thou diest; thou livest in him, and he lives in thee, and because he lives shalt thou live also: thou shalt rise in him, and thou shalt sit together in the heavenly places with him. Oh, never was husband nearer to his wife, and never head nearer to the members, and never soul nearer to the body of this flesh, than Christ is unto thee, and while it is so, think not that heaven and earth are divided. They are but kindred worlds; two ships moored close to one another, and one short plank of death will enable you to step from one into the other: this ship, all black and coaly, having done the coasting trade, the dusty business of to-day, and being full of the blackness of sorrow; and that ship all golden, with its painted pennon flying, and its sail all spread, white as the down of the sea-bird, fair as the angel's wing—I tell thee, man, the ship of heaven is moored side by side with the ship of earth, and rock though this ship may, and career though she will on stormy winds and tempests, yet the invisible and golden ship of heaven sails by her side never sundered, never divided, always ready, in order that when the hour shall come, thou mayest leap from the black, dark ship, and step upon the golden deck of that thrice happy one in which thou shalt sail for ever.

But, O man of God, there are other golden links besides this which bind the present to the future, and time unto eternity. And what are time and eternity, after all, to the believer, but like the Siamese twins, never to be separated? This earth is heaven below, the next world is but a heaven above; it is the same house —this is the lower room, and that the upper, but the same roof cover both, and the same dew falls upon each. Remember, beloved, that *the spirits of the just made perfect* are never far from you and me if we are lovers of Jesus. All those who have passed the flood have still communion with us. Do we not sing—

"The saints on earth, and all the dead,
But one communion make;
All join in Christ, the living Head,
And of his grace partake."

We have but one Head for the church triumphant and for the church militant:

"One army of the living God,
To his command we bow;
Part of the host have cross'd the flood,
And part are crossing now."

Doth not the apostle tell us that the saints above are a cloud of witnesses? After he had mentioned Abraham, and Isaac, and Jacob, and Gideon, and Barak, and Jephthah, did he not say, "Wherefore seeing we also are compassed about with so great a cloud of witnesses, let us lay aside every weight." Lo, we are running in the plains, and the glorified ones are looking down upon us. Thy mother's eyes follow thee, young man; a father's eyes are looking down upon thee, young woman. The eyes of my godly grandmother, long since glorified, I doubt not, rest on me perpetually. No doubt, in heaven they often talk of us. Methinks they sometimes visit this poor earth—they never go out of heaven, it is true, for heaven is everywhere to them. This world is to them but just one corner of God's heaven, one shady bower of paradise.

The saints of the living God, are, I doubt not, very near unto us, when we think them very far away. At any rate, they still remember us, still look f r us; for this is ever upon their hearts—the truth that they without us cannot be made perfect. They cannot be a perfect church till we are gathered in, and therefore do they long for our appearing.

But, to come to our text a little more minutely. It assures us that *the angels* have communion with us. Bright spirits, first-born sons of God, do ye think of me? Oh, cherubim, great and mighty; seraphim, burning, winged with lightning, do ye think of us? Gigantic is your stature. Our poet tells us that the wand of an angel might make a mast for some tall admiral; and doubtless he was right when he said so. Those angels of God are creatures mighty and strong, doing his commandments, hearkening to his word—and do they take notice of us? Let the Scripture answer, "Are they not all ministering spirits, sent forth to minister unto those that shall be heirs of salvation?" "The angel of the Lord encampeth round about them that fear him." "For he shall give his angels charge over thee; to keep thee in all thy ways; they shall bear thee up in their hands, lest thou dash thy foot against a stone." Yes, the brightest angels are but the serving men of the saints; they are our lacqueys and our footmen. They wait upon us; they are the troops of our body guard; and we might, if our eyes were opened, see what Elisha saw, horses of fire and chariots of fire round about us; so that we should joyously say, "More are they that are with us than they that are against us."

Our text tells us that the angels of God rejoice over repenting sinners. How is that? They are always as happy as they can be; how can they be any happier? The text does not say that they are any happier; but perhaps that they show their happiness more. A man may have a Sabbath every day, as he ought to have if he be a Christian; and yet on the first day of the week he will let his Sabbatism come out plainly; for then the world shall see that he doth rest. "A merry heart hath a continual feast;" but then even the merry heart hath some special days on which it feasteth well. To the glorified every day is a Sabbath, but of some it can be said, "and that Sabbath was an high day." There are days when the angels sing more loudly than usual; they are always harping well God's praise, but sometimes the gathering hosts who have been flitting far through the universe, come home to their centre; and round the throne of God, standing in serried ranks, marshalled not for battle but for music, on certain set and appointed days they chant the praises of the Son of God, "who loved us and gave himself for us." And do you ask me when those days occur? I tell you, the birthday of every Christian is a sonnet day in heaven. There are Christmas-days in paradise, where Christ's high mass is kept, and Christ is glorified not because he was born in a manger, but because he is born in a broken heart. There are days—good days in heaven; days of sonnet, red letter days, of overflowing adoration. And these are days when the shepherd brings home the lost sheep upon his shoulder, when the church has swept her house and found the lost piece of money; for then are these friends and neighbours called together, and they rejoice with joy unspeakable and full of glory over one sinner that repenteth.

I have thus, I hope, shown you that there is a greater connection between earth and heaven than any of us dreamed. And now let none of us think, when we look upward to the blue sky, that we are far from heaven; it is a very little distance from us. When the day comes we shall go post-haste there, even without horses and chariots of fire. Balaam called it a land that is very far off; we know better—it is a land that is very near. Even now

"By faith we join our hands
  With those that went before,
And greet the blood-besprinkled bands
  Upon the eternal shore."

All hail, bright spirits! I see you now. All hail, angels! All hail, ye brethren redeemed! A few more hours, or days, or months, and we shall join your happy throng; till then your joyous fellowship, your sweet compassion shall ever be our comfort and our consolation—and having weathered all storms of life, we shall at last anchor with you within the port of everlasting peace.

II. But the angels are said to sing whenever a sinner repents. Let us see if there is any JUDGMENT IN THEIR SONG, or whether they make a mistake. Why do angels sing over penitent sinners?

In the first place, I think it is because they remember the days of creation. You know, when God made this world, and fixed the beams of the heavens in sockets of light, the morning stars sang together, and the sons of God shouted for joy; as they saw star after star flying abroad like sparks from the great anvil of Omnipotence, they began to sing; and every time they saw a new creature made upon this little earth, they praised afresh. When first they saw light they clapped their hands, and said, "Great is Jehovah; for he said 'Light be!' and light was." And when they saw sun and moon, and stars, again they clapped their hands, and they said, "He hath made great lights; for his mercy endureth for ever. The sun to rule the day; for his mercy endureth for ever. The moon to rule the night; for his mercy endureth for ever." And over everything he made, they chanted evermore that sweet song, "Creator, thou art to be magnified; for thy mercy endureth for ever." Now, when they see a sinner returning, they see the creation over again; for repentance is a new creation. No man ever repents until God makes in him a new heart and a right spirit. I do not know that ever since the day when God made the world, with the exception of new hearts, the angels have seen God make anything else. He may, if he hath so pleased, have made fresh worlds since that time. But perhaps the only instance of new creation they have ever seen since the first day, is the creation of a new heart and a right spirit within the breast of a poor penitent sinner. Therefore do they sing, because creation cometh over again.

I doubt not, too, that they sing because they behold God's works afresh shining in excellence. When God first made the world, he said of it, "It is very good"—he could not say so now. There are many of you that God could not say that of. He would have to say the very reverse. He would have to say, "No, that is very bad, for the trail of the serpent hath swept away thy beauty, that moral excellence which once dwelt in manhood has passed away;" but when the sweet influences of the Spirit bring men to repentance and faith again, God looks upon man, and he saith, "It is very good." For what his Spirit makes is like himself—good, and holy, and precious; and God smiles again over his twice-made creation, and saith once more, "It is very good." Then the angels begin again, and praise his name, whose works are always good and full of beauty.

But, beloved, the angels sing over sinners that repent, because they know what that poor sinner has escaped. You and I can never imagine all the depths of hell. Shut out from us by a black veil of darkness, we cannot tell the horrors of that dismal dungeon of lost souls. Happily, the wailings of the damned have never startled us, for a thousand tempests were but a maiden's whisper, compared with one wail of a damned spirit. It is not possible for us to see the tortures of those souls who dwell eternally within an anguish that knows no alleviation. These eyes would become sightless balls of darkness, if they were permitted for an instant to look into that ghastly shrine of torment. Hell is horrible, for we may say of it, eye hath not seen, nor ear heard, neither hath it entered into the heart of man to conceive the horrors which God hath prepared for them that hate him. But the angels know better than you or I could guess. They know it; not that they have felt it, but they remember that day when Satan and his angels rebelled against God. They remember the day when the third part of the stars of heaven revolted against their liege Lord; and they have not forgotten how the red right hand of Jehovah Jesus was wrapt in thunder; they do not forget that breach in the battlements of heaven when, down from the greatest heights to the lowest depths, Lucifer and his hosts were hurled; they have never forgotten how, with sound of trumpet, they pursued the flying foe down to the gulphs of black despair; and, as they neared that place where the great serpent is to be bound in chains, they remember how they saw Tophet, which was prepared of old, the pile whereof is fire and much wood; and they recollect how, when they winged back their flight, every tongue was silent, although they might well have shouted the praise of him who conquered Lucifer; but on them all there did sit a solemn awe of one who could smite a cherubim, and cast him in hopeless bonds of everlasting despair. They knew what hell was, for they had looked within its jaws, and seen their own brothers, fast enclosed within them; and, therefore, when they see a sinner saved, they rejoice, because there is one less to be food for the never-dying worm—one more soul escaped out of the mouth of the lion.

There is yet a better reason. The angels know what the joys of heaven are, and therefore, they rejoice over one sinner that repenteth. We talk about pearly gates and golden streets, and white robes, and harps of gold, and crowns of amaranth, and all that; but if an angel could speak to us of heaven, he would smile and say, "All these fine things are but child's talk, and ye are little children, and ye cannot understand the greatness of eternal bliss, and therefore God has given you a child's horn book, and an alphabet, in which you may learn the first rough letters of what heaven is, but what it is thou dost not know. O mortal, thine eye hath never yet beheld its splendours; thine ear hath never yet been ravished with its melodies; thy heart has never been transported with its peerless joys." Thou mayest talk, and think, and guess, and dream, but thou canst never measure the infinite heaven which God has provided for his children: and therefore it is, when they see a soul saved and a sinner repenting, that they clap their hands; for they know that all those blessed mansions are theirs, since all those sweet places of everlasting happiness are the entail of every sinner that repenteth.

But I want you just to read the text again, while I dwell upon another thought. "There is joy in the presence of the angels of God over one sinner *that repenteth.*" Now, why do they not save their joy till that sinner dies and goes to heaven? Why do they rejoice over him when he repents? My Arminian friend, I think, ought to go to heaven, to set them right upon this matter. According to his theory, it must be very wrong of them, because they rejoice prematurely. According to the Arminian doctrine a man may repent, and yet he may be lost; he may have grace to repent and believe, and yet he may fall from grace and be a castaway. Now, angels, don't be too fast. Perhaps you may have to repent of this one day, if the Arminian doctrine be true, I would advise you to save your song for greater joys. Why, angels, perhaps the men that you are singing over to-day, you will have to mourn over to-morrow. I am quite sure that Arminius never taught his doctrine in heaven. I do not know whether he is there—I hope he is, but he is no longer an Arminian; but if he ever taught his doctrine there, he would be put out. The reason why angels rejoice is because they know that when a sinner repents, he is absolutely saved; or else they would rejoice prematurely, and would have good cause for retracting their merriment on some future occasion. But the angels know what Christ meant when he said, "I give unto my sheep eternal life, and they shall never perish, neither shall any pluck them out of my hand;" and therefore they rejoice over repenting sinners, because they know they are saved.

There is yet one more fact I will mention, before I leave this point. It is said that the angels "rejoice over *one* sinner that repenteth. Now this evening it shall be my happy privilege to give the right hand of fellowship to no less than forty-eight sinners that have repented, and there will be great joy and rejoicing in our churches to-night, because these forty-eight have been immersed on a profession of their faith. But how loving are the angels to men; for they rejoice over *one* sinner that repenteth. There she is, in that garret where the stars look between the tiles. There is a miserable bed in that room, with but one bit of covering, and she lieth there to die! Poor creature! many a night she has walked the streets in the time of her merriment; but now her joys are over; a foul disease, like a demon, is devouring her heart! She is dying fast, and no one careth for her soul! But there, in that chamber, she turns her face to the wall, and she cries, "O thou that savedst Magdalene, save me; Lord I repent; have mercy upon me; I beseech thee." Did the bells ring in the street? Was the trumpet blown? Ah! no. Did men rejoice? Was there a sound of thanksgiving in the midst of the great congregation? No; no one heard it; for she died unseen. But stay! There was one standing at her bedside, who noted well that tear; an angel, who had come down from heaven to watch over this stray sheep, and mark its return; and no sooner was her prayer uttered than he clapped his wings, and there was seen flying up to the pearly gates a spirit like a star. The heavenly guards came crowding to the gate, crying, "What news, O son of fire?" He said, "'Tis done." "And what is done?" they said, "Why, she has repented." "What! she who was once a chief of sinners? has she turned to Christ?" "'Tis even so," said he. And then they told it through the streets, and the bells of heaven rang marriage peals, for Magdalene was saved, and she who had been the chief of sinners was turned unto the living God.

It was in another place. A poor neglected little boy in ragged clothing had run about the streets for many a-day. Tutored in crime, he was paving his path to the gallows; but one morning he passed by a humble room, where some men and women were sitting together teaching poor ragged children. He stepped in there, a wild Bedouin of the streets; they talked to him; they told him about a soul and about an eternity—things he had never heard before; they spoke of Jesus, and of good tidings of great joy to this poor friendless lad. He went another Sabbath, and another; his wild habits hanging about him, for he could not get rid of them. At last it happened that his teacher said to him one day, "Jesus Christ receiveth sinners." That little boy ran, but not home, for it was but a mockery to call it so—where a drunken father and a lascivious mother kept a hellish riot together. He ran, and under some dry arch, or in some wild unfrequented corner, he bent his little knees, and there he cried, that poor creature in his rags, "Lord save me, or I perish;" and the little Arab was on his knees—the little thief was saved! He said—

"Jesus, lover of my soul, let me to thy bosom fly;"

And up from that old arch, from that forsaken hovel, there flew a spirit, glad to bear the news to heaven, that another heir of glory was born to God. I might picture many such scenes; but will each of you try to picture your own? You remember the occasion when the Lord met with you. Ah! little did you think what a commotion there was in heaven. If the Queen had ordered out all her soldiers, the angels of heaven would not have stopped to notice them; if all the princes of earth had marched in pageant through the streets, with all their robes, and jewellery, and crowns, and all their regalia, their chariots, and their horsemen—if the pomps of ancient monarchies had risen from the tomb—if all the might of Babylon and Tyre and Greece had been concentrated into one great parade, yet not an angel would have stopped in his course to smile at those poor tawdry things; but over you the vilest of the vile, the poorest of the poor, the most obscure and unknown—over you angelic wings were hovering, and concerning you it was said on earth and sung in heaven, "Hallelujah, for a child is born to God to-day."

III. And now I must conclude with this LESSON TO THE SAINTS. I think, beloved, it will not be hard for you to learn. The angels of heaven rejoice over sinners that repent: saints of God, will not you and I do the same? I do not think the church rejoices enough. We all grumble enough and groan enough: but very few of us rejoice enough. When we take a large number into the church it is spoken of as a great mercy; but is the greatness of that mercy appreciated? I will tell you who they are that can most appreciate the conversion of sinners. They are those that are just converted themselves, or those that have been great sinners themselves. Those who have been saved themselves from bondage, when they see others coming who have so lately worn the chains, are so glad that they can well take the tabret, and the harp, and the pipe, and the psaltery, and praise God that there are other prisoners who have been emancipated by grace. But there are others who can do this better still, and they are the parents and relations of those who are saved. You have thanked God many times when you have seen a sinner saved; but, mother did not you thank him most when you saw your son converted? Oh! those holy tears; they are not tears—they are God's diamonds—the tears of a mother's joy, when her son confesses his faith in Jesus. Oh! that glad countenance of the wife, when she sees her husband, long bestial and drunken, at last made into a man and a Christian! Oh! that look of joy which a young Christian gives, when he sees his father converted, who had long oppressed and persecuted him. I was preaching this week for a young minister, and being anxious to know his character, I spoke of him with apparent coolness to an estimable lady of his congregation. In a very few moments she began to warm in his favour. She said, "You must not say anything against him, sir; if you do, it is because you do not know him." "Oh," I said, "I knew him long before you did; he is not much, is he?" "Well," she said, "I must speak well of him, for he has been a blessing to my servants and family." I went out into the street, and saw some men and women standing about; so I said to them, "I must take your minister away" "If you do," they said, "we will follow you all over the world, if you take away a man who has done so much good to our souls." After collecting the testimony of fifteen or sixteen witnesses, I said, "If the man gets such witnesses as these let him go on; the Lord has opened his mouth, and the devil will never be able to shut it." These are the witnesses we want—men who can sing with the angels because their own households are converted to God. I hope it may be so with all of you; and if any of you are yourselves brought to Christ to-day—for he is willing to receive you—you will go out of this place singing, and the angels will sing with you. There shall be joy in earth, and joy in heaven; on earth peace, and glory to God in the highest. The Lord bless you one and all, for Jesus' sake.

Metropolitan Tabernacle Pulpit.

THE PRODIGAL'S CLIMAX.

A Sermon

INTENDED FOR READING ON LORD'S-DAY, MAY 26TH, 1895,

DELIVERED BY

C. H. SPURGEON,

AT THE METROPOLITAN TABERNACLE, NEWINGTON,

On Thursday Evening, May 19th, 1887.

"When he came to himself."—Luke xv. 17.

THERE are different stages in the sinner's history, and they are worth marking in the prodigal's experience. There is, first, the stage in which the young man sought independence of his father. The younger son said, "Father, give me the portion of goods that falleth to me." We know something of that state of mind; and, alas! it is a very common one. As yet there is no open profligacy, no distinct rebellion against God. Religious services are attended, the father's God is held in reverence; but in his heart the young man desires a supposed liberty, he wishes to cast off all restraint. Companions hint that he is too much tied to his mother's apron-string. He himself feels that there may be some strange delights which he has never enjoyed; and the curiosity of Mother Eve to taste the fruit of that tree which was good for food, and pleasant to the eyes, and a tree to be desired to make one wise, comes into the young man's mind, and he wishes to put forth his hand, and take the fruit of the tree of the knowledge of good and evil, that he may eat thereof. He never intends to spend his substance in riotous living, but he would like to have the opportunity of spending it as he likes. He does not mean to be a profligate; still, he would like to have the honour of choosing what is right on his own account. At any rate, he is a man now; he feels his blushing honours full upon him, and he wants now to exercise his own freedom of will, and to feel that he himself is really his own master. Who, indeed, he asks, is Lord over him? Perhaps there are some to whom I am speaking who are just in such a state as that; if so, may the grace of God arrest you before you go any further away from him! May you feel that, to be out of gear with God, to wish to be separated from him, and to have other interests than those of him who made you, must be dangerous, and probably will be fatal! Therefore now, even now, may you come to yourself at this earliest stage of your history, and also come to love and rejoice in God as the prodigal returned to his father!

Very soon, however, this young man in the parable entered upon quite another stage. He had received his portion of goods; all that he would have had at his father's death he had turned into ready money, and there it is. It is his own, and he may do what he pleases with it. Having already indulged his independent feeling towards his father, and his wish to have a separate establishment altogether from him, he knew that he would be freer to carry out his plans if he was right away. Anywhere near his father there is a check upon him; he feels that the influence of his home somewhat clips his wings. If he could get into a far country, there he should have the opportunity to develop; and all that evolution could do for him he would have the opportunity of enjoying, so he gathers all together, and goes into the far country. It may be that I am addressing some who have reached that stage. Now there is all the delirium of self-indulgence. Now it is all gaiety, "a short life and a merry one," forgetting the long eternity and a woful one. Now the cup is full, and the red wine sparkles in the bowl. As yet, it has not bitten you like a serpent, nor stung you like an adder, as it will do all too soon; but just now, it is the deadly sweetness that you taste, and the exhilaration of that drugged chalice that deceives you. You are making haste to enjoy yourself. Sin is a dangerous joy, beloved all the more because of the danger; for, where there is a fearful risk, there is often an intense pleasure to a daring heart; and you perhaps are one of that venturous band, spending your days in folly and your nights in riotousness.

Ere long there comes a third stage to the sinner as well as to the prodigal, that is when he has "spent all." We have only a certain amount of spending money after all. He who has gold without limit, yet has not health without limit; or if health does not fail him in his sinning, yet desire fails, and satiety comes in, as it did with Solomon when he tried this way of seeking happiness. At last, there is no honey left, there is only the sting of the bee. At last, there is no sweetness in the cup, there is only the delirium that follows the intoxication. At last, the meat is eaten to the bone, and there is nothing good to come out of that bone; it contains no marrow, the teeth are broken with it, and the man wishes that he had never sat down to so terrible a feast. He has reached the stage at which the prodigal arrived when he had spent all. Oh, there be some who spend all their character, spend all their health and strength, spend all their hope, spend all their uprightness, spend everything that was worth having! They have spent all. This is another stage in the sinner's history, and it is very apt to lead to despair, and even deeper sin, and sometimes to that worst of sins which drives a man red-handed before the bar of his Maker to account for his own blood.

It is a dreadful state to be in, for there comes at the back of it a terrible hunger. There is a weary labour to get something that may stay the spirit, a descending to the degradation of feeding swine, a willingness to eat of the husks that swine do eat, yet an inability to do so. Many have felt this craving that cannot be satisfied. But, for my part, I am glad when "the rake's progress" has reached this point; for often, in the grace of God, it is the way home for the prodigal; it is a roundabout way, but it is the way home for him. When men have spent all, and poverty has followed on their recklessness, and sickness has come at the call of their vice, then it is that omnipotent grace has stepped in, and there has come another stage in the sinner's history, of which I am now going to speak, as God may help me. That is the point the prodigal had reached "when he came to himself."

I. Then, first, A SINNER IS BESIDE HIMSELF.

While he is living in his sin, he is out of his mind, he is beside himself. I am sure that it is so. There is nothing more like to madness than sin; and it is a moot point among those who study deep problems how far insanity and the tendency to sin go side by side, and whereabouts it is that great sin and entire loss of responsibility may touch each other. I do not intend to discuss that question at all; but I am going to say that every sinner is morally and responsibly insane, and therefore in a worse condition than if he were only mentally insane.

He is insane, first, because *his judgment is altogether out of order.* He makes fatal mistakes about all-important matters. He reckons a short time of this mortal life to be worth all his thoughts, and he puts eternity into the background. He considers it possible for a creature to be at enmity against the Creator, or indifferent to him, and yet to be happy. He fancies that he knows better what is right for him than the law of God declares. He dreams that the everlasting gospel, which cost God the life of his own Son, is scarcely worthy of his attention at all, and he passes it by with contempt. He has unshipped the rudder of his judgment, and steers towards the rocks with awful deliberation, and seems as if he would wish to know where he can find the surest place to commit eternal shipwreck. His judgment is out of order.

Further, *his actions are those of a madman.* This prodigal son, first of all, had interests apart from his father. He must have been mad to have conceived such an idea as that. For me to have interests apart from him who made me, and keeps me alive,—for me, the creature of an hour, to fancy that I can have a will in opposition to the will of God, and that I can so live and prosper,—why, I must be a fool! I must be mad to wish any such thing, for it is consistent with the highest reason to believe that he who yields himself up to omnipotent goodness must be in the track of happiness, but that he who sets himself against the almighty grace of God must certainly be kicking against the pricks to his own wounding and hurt. Yet this sinner does not see that it is so, and the reason is that he is beside himself.

Then, next, that young man went away from his home, though it was the best home in all the world. We can judge that from the exceeding tenderness and generosity of the father at the head of it, and from the wonderful way in which all the servants had such entire sympathy with their master. It was a happy home, well stored with all that the son could need; yet he quits it to go he knows not whither, among strangers who did not care a straw for him, and who, when they had drained his purse, would not give him even a penny with which to buy bread to save him from starving. The prodigal must have been mad to act like that; and for any of us to leave him who has been the dwelling-place of his saints in all generations, to quit the warmth and comfort of the Church of God which is the home of joy and peace, is clear insanity. Anyone who does this is acting against his own best interests, he is choosing the path of shame and sorrow, he is casting away all true delight; he must be mad.

You can see that this young man is out of his mind, because, when he gets into the far country, he begins spending his money riotously. He does not lay it out judiciously, he spends his money for that which is not bread, and his labour for that which satisfieth not; and that is just what the sinner does. If he be self-righteous, he is trying to weave a robe out of the worthless material of his own works; and if he be a voluptuary, given up to sinful indulgence, what vanity it is for him to hope for pleasure in the midst of sin! Should I expect to meet with angels in the sewers, with heavenly light in a dark mine? Nay, these are not places for such things as those; and can I rationally look for joy to my heart from revelling, chambering, wantonness, and such conduct? If I do, I must be mad. Oh, if men were but rational,—and they often wrongly suppose that they are,—if they were but rational beings, they would see how irrational it is to sin! The most reasonable thing in the world is to spend life for its own true design, and not to fling it away as though it were a pebble on the sea-shore.

Further, the prodigal was a fool, he was mad, for he spent all. He did not even stop half way on the road to penury, but he went on till he had spent all. There is no limit to those who have started in a course of sin. He that stays back from it, by God's grace may keep from it; but it is with sin as it is with the intoxicating cup. One said to me, the other day, "I can drink much, or I can drink none; but I have not the power to drink a little, for if I begin I cannot stop myself, and may go to any length." So is it with sin, God's grace can keep you abstaining from sin; but, if you begin sinning, oh, how one sin draws on another! One sin is the decoy or magnet for another sin, and draws it on; and one cannot tell, when he begins to descend this slippery slide, how quickly and how far he may go. Thus the prodigal spent all in utter recklessness; and, oh, the recklessness of some young sinners whom I know! And, oh, the greater recklessness of some old sinners who seem resolved to be damned, for, having but a little remnant of life left, they waste that last fragment of it in fatal delay!

Then it was, dear friends, when the prodigal had spent all, that he still further proved his madness. That would have been the time to go home to his father; but, apparently, that thought did not occur to him. "He went and joined himself to a citizen of that country," still overpowered by the fascination that kept him away from the one place where he might have been happy; and that is one of the worst proofs of the madness of some of you who frequent these courts, that, though you know about the great God and his infinite mercy, and know somewhat of how much you need him and his grace, yet you still try to get what you want somewhere else, and do not go back to him.

I shall not have time to say much more upon this point, but I must remind you that, like sinners, *the prodigal had the ways of a madman.* I have had, at times, to deal with those whose reason has failed them, and I have noticed that many of them have been perfectly sane, and even wise and clever, on all points except one. So is it with the sinner. He is a famous politician; just hear him talk. He is a wonderful man of business; see how sharply he looks after every penny. He is very judicious in everything but this, he is mad on one point, he has a fatal monomania, for it concerns his own soul.

A madman will often conceal his madness from those round about him; so will a sinner hide his sin. You may talk with this man about morals, and you may watch him very closely; yet you may be a long time before you can find him out, and be able to say to him, "One thing thou lackest." Perhaps, on a sudden, you touch that weak point, and there he stands fully developed before you, far gone in his insanity. He is right enough elsewhere, but with regard to his soul his reason is gone.

Mad people do not know that they have been mad till they are cured; they think that they alone are wise, and all the rest are fools. Here is another point of their resemblance to sinners, for they also think that everybody is wrong except themselves. Hear how they will abuse a pious wife as "a fool." What hard words they will use towards a gracious daughter! How they will rail at the ministers of the gospel, and try to tear God's Bible to pieces! Poor mad souls, they think all are mad except themselves! We, with tears, pray God to deliver them from their delusions, and to bring them to sit at the feet of Jesus, clothed, and in their right minds.

Sometimes, the sinner will be seen and known to be mad because he turns on his best friends, as madmen do. Those whom they otherwise would have loved the most they reckon to be their worst enemies. So God, who is man's best Friend, is most despised, and Christ, who is the Friend of sinners, is rejected, and the most earnest Christians are often the most avoided or persecuted by sinners.

Mad people sometimes, too, will rave, and then you know what dreadful things they will say. So is it with sinners when their fits are on them. I dare not speak of what they will do and what they will say. They often pull themselves up, afterwards, and feel ashamed to think that they should have gone so far; yet so it is, for they are beside themselves, even as the prodigal was.

I will not dwell longer on this sad fact, because I want to speak on the next and brighter part of my theme.

II. Secondly, IT IS A BLESSED THING WHEN THE SINNER COMES TO HIMSELF: "When he came to himself." This is the first mark of grace working in the sinner as it was the first sign of hope for the prodigal.

Sometimes, *this change occurs suddenly.* I was greatly charmed, this week, by meeting with one to whom this happened. It was an old-fashioned sort of conversion, with which I was delighted. There came into this building, some three months ago, a man who had not for a long time gone to any place of worship. He despised such things; he could swear, and drink, and do worse things still, he was careless, godless; but he had a mother who often prayed for him, and he had a brother who is, I believe, here to-night, whose prayer has never ceased for him. He did not come here to worship, he came just to see the preacher whom his brother had been hearing for so many years; but, coming in, somehow he was no sooner in the place than he felt that he was unfit to be here, so he went up into the top gallery, as far back as he could, and when some friend beckoned him to take a seat, he felt that he could not do so, he must just lean against the wall at the back. Someone else invited him to sit down, but he could not; he felt that he had no right to do so; but when the preacher announced his text,*—"And the publican, standing afar off, would not lift up so much as his eyes unto heaven, but smote upon his breast, saying, God be merciful to me a sinner;"—and said something like this, "You that stand farthest off in the Tabernacle, and dare not sit down because you feel your guilt to be so great, you are the man to whom God has sent me this morning, and he bids you come to Christ and find mercy," a miracle of love was wrought. Then, "he came to himself," as he will tell us soon at the church-meeting, when he comes forward to confess his faith. I rejoiced greatly when I heard of it, for in his case there is a change that everybody who knows him can see. He has become full of a desire after everything that is gracious as once he practised everything that was bad. Now that is what sometimes happens, and why should it not happen again to-night? Why should not some other man, or some woman, come to himself or to herself to-night? This is the way home, first to come to yourself, and then to come to your God. "He came to himself."

On the other hand, sometimes *this change is very gradual.* I need not dwell upon that, but there are many who have their eyes opened by degrees. They first see men as trees walking; afterwards, they see all things clearly. So long as they do but come to themselves, and come to the Saviour, I mind not how they come. Some conversions are sudden, some gradual; but in every case, if it be the work of the Holy Spirit, and the man comes to himself, it is well.

Now let us consider *how this change happened.* If you should ask me the outward circumstances of the prodigal's case, I should say that it took a great deal to bring him to himself. "Why, surely!" one says, "he ought to have come to himself when he had spent all, he must have come to himself when he began to be hungry." No; it took a great deal to bring him to himself, and to his father; and it takes a great deal to bring sinners to themselves, and to their God. There are some of you who will have to be beaten with many stripes before you will be saved. I heard one say, who was crushed almost to death in an accident, "If I had not nearly perished, I should have wholly perished." So is it with many sinners; if some had not lost

* See *Metropolitan Tabernacle Pulpit*, No. 1,949, "A Sermon for the Worst Man on Earth."

all they had, they would have lost all; but, by strong winds, rough and raging, some are driven into the port of peace.

The occasion of the prodigal's climax was this; he was very hungry, and in great sorrow, and he was alone. It is a grand thing if we can get people to be alone. There was nobody near the poor man, and no sound for him to hear except the grunting of the hogs, and the munching of those husks. Ah, to be alone! I wish that we had more opportunities of being alone in this great city; yet, perhaps the most awful loneliness may be realized while walking a London street. It is a good thing for a sinner sometimes to be alone. The prodigal had nobody to drink with him, nobody to sport with him; he was too far gone for that. He had not a rag to pawn to get another pint, he must therefore just sit still without one of his old companions. They only followed him for what they could get out of him. As long as he could treat them, they would treat him well; but when he had spent all, "no man gave unto him." He was left without a comrade, in misery he could not allay, in hunger he could not satisfy. He pulled that belt up another hole, and made it tighter; but it almost seemed as if he would pull himself in two if he drew it any closer. He was reduced almost to a skeleton; emaciation had taken hold of him, and he was ready to lie down there and die. Then it was that he came to himself.

Do you know *why this change occurred in the prodigal's case?* I believe that the real reason was that his father was secretly working for him all the while. His state was known to his father; I am sure it was, because the elder brother knew it; and if the elder brother heard of it, so did the father. The elder brother may have told him; or, if not, the father's greater love would have a readier ear for tidings of his son than the elder brother had. Though the parable cannot tell us,—for no parable is meant to teach us everything,—yet it was true that the Father was omnipotent, and he was secretly touching the core of this young man's heart, and dealing with him by this wondrous surgery of famine and of want to make him at last come to himself.

Perhaps somebody here says, "I wish I could come to myself, sir, without going through all that process." Well, you have come to yourself already if you really wish that. Let me suggest to you that, in order to prove that it is so, you should begin seriously to think, to think about who you are, and where you are, and what is to become of you. Take time to think, and think in an orderly, steady, serious manner; and, if you can, jot down your thoughts. It is a wonderful help to some people to put down upon paper an account of their own condition. I believe that there were many who found the Saviour one night when I urged them, when they went home, to write on a piece of paper, "Saved as a believer in Jesus," or else, "Condemned because I believe not on the Son of God." Some who began to write that word "condemned" have never finished it, for they found Christ there and then while seeking him. You keep your account books, do you not? I am sure you do if you are in trade, unless you are going to cheat your creditors. You keep your business books; well, now, keep a record concerning your soul. Really look these matters in the face, the hereafter, death which may come so suddenly, the great eternity, the judgment-seat. Do think about these things; do not shut your eyes to them. Men and women, I pray you, do not play the fool! If you must play the fool, take some lighter things to trifle with than your souls, and your eternal destinies. Shut yourselves up alone for a while; go through this matter steadily, lay it out in order, make a plan of it. See where you are going. Think over the way of salvation, the story of the cross, the love of God, the readiness of Christ to save; and I think that, while this process is going on, you will feel your heart melting, and soon you will find your soul believing in the precious blood which sets the sinner free.

III. I had much more to say, but time has gone; so I must close with just a few words on this last point, WHEN HE CAME TO HIMSELF, THEN HE CAME TO HIS FATHER.

When a sinner comes to himself, he soon comes to his God. This poor prodigal, soon after he came to himself, said, "I will arise, and go to my father." What led him back to his father? Very briefly let me answer that question.

First, *his memory aroused him.* He recollected his father's house, he remembered the past, his own riotous living. Do not try to forget all that has happened; the terrible recollections of a misspent past may be the means of leading you to a new life. Set memory to work.

Next, *his misery bestirred him.* Every pang of hunger that he felt, the sight of his rags, the degradation of associating with swine,—all those things drove him back to his father. O sirs, let your very needs, your cravings, your misery, drive you to your God!

Then, *his fears whipped him back.* He said, "I perish with hunger." He had not perished yet, but he was afraid that he soon would do so; he feared that he really would die, for he felt so faint. O sirs, see what will become of you if you do die in your sins! What awaits you but an endless future of limitless misery? Sin will follow you into eternity, and will increase upon you there, and as you shall go on to sin, so shall you go on to sorrow ever-increasing. A deeper degradation and a more tremendous penalty will accompany your sin in the world to come; therefore, let your fears drive you home, as they drove home the poor prodigal.

Meanwhile, *his hope drew him.* This gentle cord was as powerful as the heavy whip: "In my father's house there is bread enough and to spare; I need not perish with hunger, I may yet be filled." Oh, think of what you may yet be! Poor sinner, think of what God can do and is ready to do for you, to do for you even to-night! How happy he can make you! How peaceful and how blessed! So let your hope draw you to him.

Then, *his resolve moved him.* He said, "I will arise, and go to my father." All else drove him or drew him, and now he is resolved to return home. He rose up from the earth on which he had been sitting amidst his filthiness, and he said, "I will." Then the man became a man; he had come to himself, the manhood had come back to him, and he said, "I will, I will."

Lastly, there was the real act of going to his father; it was that which brought him home. Nay, let me correct myself; it is said, "*He came to his father*," but there is a higher truth at the back of that, for *his father came to him.* So, when you are moved to return, and the resolution becomes an action, and you arise, and go to God, salvation is yours almost before you could have expected it; for, once turn your face that way, and while you are yet a great way off, your Father will outstrip the wind, and come and meet you, and fall upon your neck, and kiss you with the kisses of reconciliation. This shall be your portion if you will but trust the Lord Jesus Christ.

As for you, Christian people, who may be saying that there is nothing for you in the sermon, do not turn into a company of grumbling elder brothers; but, on the contrary, go home, and pray God to bless this discourse. "But," you say, "I have not had the fatted calf to-night." "Oh, but if it was killed for the younger son, it was for you also!" "I did not have the music and dancing to-night." Well, they have had it over the returned prodigal, over some soul that has already believed in Christ to-night; I know they have, God does not let us preach for nought. He will pay us our wages, and give us our reward; so rejoice with us over all that the Lord has done, and all that he is going to do. The Lord bless you, beloved, all of you, without exception, for Christ's sake! Amen.

Exposition by C. H. Spurgeon.

LUKE XV.

This is a chapter that needs no explanation; it carries its key within itself, and the experience of every child of God is the best exposition of it. The three parables recorded here set forth the work of saving grace in different aspects.

Verses 1, 2. *Then drew near unto him all the publicans and sinners for to hear him. And the Pharisees and scribes murmured, saying, This man receiveth sinners, and eateth with them.*

The Pharisees and scribes formed the outside ring of Christ's hearers, but the inner circle consisted of the guilty, the heavy-laden, and the lowly. They pressed as near to Christ as they could, that they might catch his every word; and besides, there was an attractiveness about his manner that drew them towards him. His mercy attracted their misery. They wanted him, and he desired them; they were thus well met. There will be an inner circle to-night when the gospel is preached, and it will not consist of the self-righteous. They that are full will not press to the table on which the gospel feast is spread, the hungry will be found nearest to the heavenly provision.

3. *And he spake this parable unto them, saying,*

There are three parables here; but, inasmuch as it is called "this parable", it is really only one. It is a picture in three panels, representing the same scene from different points of view.

4. *What man of you, having an hundred sheep, if he lose one of them, doth not leave the ninety and nine in the wilderness, and go after that which is lost, until he find it?*

It has a new importance in his eyes, for it is lost. Before, it was only one of a hundred in the fold; but now it is one distinct and separate from all the rest, and the shepherd's thought is fixed upon it.

5, 6. *And when he hath found it, he layeth it on his shoulders, rejoicing. And when he cometh home, he calleth together his friends and neighbours, saying unto them, Rejoice with me; for I have found my sheep which was lost.*

No doubt he was glad that the other sheep were not lost; but that joy was, for a while, quite eclipsed in the more striking and vivid joy over the one which had been lost.

7. *I say unto you, that likewise joy shall be in heaven over one sinner that repenteth, more than over ninety and nine just persons, which need no repentance.*

If such there be,—and there are many who think that they belong to this class,—they bring no joy to the great Shepherd; but you who have had to mourn over your lost estate set the bells of heaven ringing with a new melody when you are recovered by the great Redeemer.

The first of these three parables may be said to represent salvation in reference to the work of the Son of God as the great Seeker and Saver of the souls of men. In the second, we have a representation of the work of the Holy Spirit in the Church of God.

8. *Either what woman having ten pieces of silver, if she lose one piece, doth not light a candle, and sweep the house, and seek diligently till she find it?*

Her thoughts were all concerning that one lost piece. It had not more intrinsic value than the rest, but being lost it called off her attention from the other nine. She valued it, and for the hope of finding it she lighted a candle, swept the house, and sought diligently till she found it. This is a picture of the Holy Spirit's work in seeking for lost souls. They bear the King's impress, they are coins of the realm. This woman knew that the silver coin was not far away, so she swept the house, and sought diligently, using all her eyes, devoting all her time to this one object, quitting all other avocations until she found it.

9. *And when she hath found it, she calleth her friends and her neighbours together, saying, Rejoice with me; for I have found the piece which I had lost.*

She might never have called them together to rejoice that she had ten pieces of silver, she might even have hidden them away; and the joy she had in them might have been only her own, a solitary joy; but now that one piece had been lost, and had been found again, she says, "Rejoice with me; for I have found the piece which I had lost."

10. *Likewise, I say unto you, there is joy in the presence of the angels of God over one sinner that repenteth.*

Not joy among the angels, as some read it, though no doubt that is a truth; but "joy in the presence of the angels of God;" and what can that mean but that God himself rejoices, and rejoices so that angels perceive it; and no doubt they then join in the delight? But all this points out that it is the lost one that is the great object of consideration, that out of any congregation where the gospel is preached, it is the lost one who is the most important person in the whole place.

In the next verses, we get the Father's part in the work of the recovery of the wanderer.

11—13. *And he said, A certain man had two sons: and the younger of them said to his father, Father, give me the portion of goods that falleth to me. And he divided unto them his living. And not many days after the younger son gathered all together, and took his journey into a far country, and there wasted his substance with riotous living.*

His heart was far away when he asked his father to give him his portion; and now his body is far away as he goes into the outward wandering which follows after the inner wandering.

14. *And when he had spent all, there arose a mighty famine in that land;*

There generally does arise "a mighty famine" in such cases. Famines and other miseries are God's messengers which he sends after his wandering children.

14. *And he began to be in want.*

This was a new sensation to him; he had never known it when he was at home. He did not know it in his first boisterous days away from his father's house, but now "he began to be in want."

15. *And he went and joined himself to a citizen of that country; and he sent him into his fields to feed swine.*

Perhaps he did not want to employ him, but said that he would give him that occupation if he cared to accept it. It was small pay, very dishonouring work to a Jew, not fit employment for the son of a nobleman; yet "half a loaf is better than no bread," so he took it, though even the half loaf must have been a very small one.

16. *And he would fain have filled his belly with the husks that the swine did eat: and no man gave unto him.*

Such a thing as generosity was not known in that country. His companions could share his riches when he was living riotously, but they will not share their riches now that he is in his poverty.

17. *And when he came to himself, he said, How many hired servants of my father's have bread enough and to spare, and I perish with hunger!*

"My father's day-labourers have bread enough and to spare, yet I, his child, perish with hunger."

18, 19. *I will arise and go to my father, and will say unto him, Father, I have sinned against heaven, and before thee, and am no more worthy to be called thy son: make me as one of thy hired servants.*

You notice that this last part of the prayer he never did pray; for it was stopped by his father's love. There was a legalism about it naturally suggested by his own despair, but it was not such as his father would tolerate.

20, 21. *And he arose, and came to his father. But when he was yet a great way off, his father saw him, and had compassion, and ran, and fell on his neck, and kissed him. And the son said unto him, Father, I have sinned against heaven, and in thy sight, and am no more worthy to be called thy son.*

There comes an interruption there; the kiss upon his lips stops the rest of the prayer which he had prepared, and now the father declares his will concerning the wanderer.

22—24. *But the father said to his servants, Bring forth the best robe, and put it on him; and put a ring on his hand, and shoes on his feet: and bring hither the fatted calf, and kill it; and let us eat, and be merry: for this my son was dead, and is alive again; he was lost, and is found. And they began to be merry.*

I have never read that they left off being merry, for the conversion of a soul is enough to make eternal joy in the hearts of the righteous.

25, 26. *Now his elder son was in the field: and as he came and drew nigh to the house, he heard musick and dancing. And he called one of the servants, and asked what these things meant.*

This was a new thing, and apparently a thing that he did not care much about. How had it come to pass that there was such noise, such joy?

27, 28. *And he said unto him, Thy brother is come; and thy father hath killed the fatted calf, because he hath received him safe and sound. And he was angry, and would not go in: therefore came his father out, and intreated him.*

I hardly know which to admire most, the love of the father when he fell upon the neck of the prodigal, or the love of the father when he went out to talk with his elder son: "Therefore came his father out, and intreated him." Oh, our God is very good to us when we give way to naughty tempers! If we begin to think that we are very holy people, that we have been long the servants of God, and that there ought to be some little fuss made over us as well as over great sinners that come into the church, then our Father is very gentle, and he comes out and entreats us.

29. *And he answering said to his father, Lo, these many years do I serve thee, neither transgressed I at any time thy commandment: and yet thou never gavest me a kid, that I might make merry with my friends:*

"I have had no banquets. I have kept at home, a patient worker, and have had no extraordinary joys." I know some Christian workers who are very much in this condition. They keep on and on and on in holy service, and they do well; but they seldom have great entertainments of high joy and unspeakable delight. It is their own fault, and it is a thousand pities that they do not have them, for they might have them if they would. There is a tendency to grow so absorbed in service, like Martha, that we are cumbered by it; and we do not have the joy of Mary in communion at the Master's feet. I am sure that this elder son was out of fellowship with his father, or else he would not have talked as he did. We are all apt to get into such a condition. See to it, ye who work for Jesus, that it is not so with you.

Then the elder brother went on to say,—

30. *But as soon as this thy son was come, which hath devoured thy living with harlots, thou hast killed for him the fatted calf.*

I do not read that the prodigal had devoured his father's living with harlots; that is the elder brother's version of it. I dare say that it was true, but it is always a pity to give the roughest interpretation to things. He had spent his substance "in riotous living." When we are cross, we generally use the ugliest words we can; we may think that we are speaking forcibly, but indeed we are speaking naughtily, and not as our Father would have us speak.

31. *And he said unto him, Son, thou art ever with me, and all that I have is thine.*

Oh, what a word was that! How it reminds Christians of their privileges, if they would but appropriate them! It is yours, beloved, to live always with your God, and to know that all that he has is yours. You ought to live in a perpetual festival; for you there should be one joyful Christmas-tide that lasts from the beginning of the year to the end of it: "Son, thou art ever with me, and all that I have is thine."

32. *It was meet that we should make merry, and be glad: for this thy brother was dead, and is alive again; and was lost, and is found.*

It was the fit thing, and the proper thing, and the right thing, that there should be extraordinary joy over a returning sinner. There ought to be, there must be, there shall be, special music and dancing over sinners saved by the grace of God. The Lord give us some such to-night, and make us glad over them! Amen.

Metropolitan Tabernacle Pulpit.

NUMBER ONE THOUSAND; OR, "BREAD ENOUGH AND TO SPARE."

A Sermon

DELIVERED ON LORD'S-DAY MORNING, JULY 16TH, 1871, BY

C. H. SPURGEON,

AT THE METROPOLITAN TABERNACLE, NEWINGTON.

"And when he came to himself, he said, How many hired servants of my father's have bread enough and to spare, and I perish with hunger!"—Luke xv. 17.

"HE came to himself." The word may be applied to one waking out of a deep swoon. He had been unconscious of his true condition, and he had lost all power to deliver himself from it; but now he was coming round again, returning to consciousness and action. The voice which shall awaken the dead aroused him; the visions of his sinful trance all disappeared; his foul but fascinating dreams were gone; he came to himself. Or the word may be applied to one recovering from insanity. The prodigal son had played the madman, for sin is madness of the worst kind. He had been demented, he had put bitter for sweet and sweet for bitter, darkness for light and light for darkness; he had injured himself, and had done for his soul what those possessed of devils in our Saviour's time did for their bodies, when they wounded themselves with stones, and cut themselves with knives. The insane man does not know himself to be insane, but as soon as he comes to himself he painfully perceives the state from which he is escaping. Returning then to true reason and sound judgment, the prodigal came to himself. Another illustration of the word may be found in the old world fables of enchantment: when a man was disenthralled from the magician's spell he "came to himself." Classic story has its legend of Circe, the enchantress, who transformed men into swine. Surely this young man in our parable had been degraded in the same manner. He had lowered his manhood to the level of the brutes. It should be the property of man to have love to his kindred, to have respect for right, to have some care for his own interest; this young man had lost all these proper attributes of humanity, and so had become as the beast that perisheth. But as the poet sings of Ulysses, that he compelled the enchantress to restore his companions to their original form, so here we see the prodigal returning to manhood, looking away from his sensual pleasures, and commencing a course of conduct more consistent with his birth and parentage. There are men here to-day perhaps who are still in this swoon; O God of heaven, arouse them! Some here who are morally insane; the Lord recover them, the divine Physician put his cooling hand upon their fevered brow, and say to them: "I will; be thou made whole." Perhaps there are others here who have allowed their animal nature to reign supreme; may he who destroys the works of the devil deliver them from the power of Satan, and give them power to become the sons of God. He shall have all the glory!

It appears that when the prodigal came to himself he was shut up to two thoughts. Two facts were clear to him, that there was plenty in his father's house, and that he himself was famishing. May the two kindred spiritual facts have absolute power over all your hearts, if you are yet unsaved; for they were most certainly all-important and pressing truths. These are no fancies of one in a dream; no ravings of a maniac; no imaginations of one under fascination: it is most true that there is plenty of all good things in the Father's house, and that the sinner needs them. No where else can grace be found or pardon gained; but with God there is plenitude of mercy; let none venture to dispute this glorious truth. Equally true is it that the sinner without God is perishing. He is perishing now; he will perish everlastingly. All that is worth having in his existence will be utterly destroyed, and he himself shall only remain as a desolation; the owl and the bittern of misery and anguish shall haunt the ruins of his nature for ever and for ever. If we could shut up unconverted men to those two thoughts, what hopeful congregations we should have. Alas! they forget that there is mercy only with God, and fancy that it is to be found somewhere else; and they try to slip away from the humbling fact of their own lost estate, and imagine that perhaps there may be some back door of escape; that, after all, they are not so bad as the Scripture declares, or that perchance it shall be right with them at the last, however wrong it may be with them now. Alas! my brethren, what shall we do with those who wilfully shut their eyes to truths of which the evidence is overwhelming, and the importance overpowering? I earnestly entreat those of you who know how to approach the throne of God in faith, to breathe the prayer that he would now bring into captivity the unconverted heart, and put these two strong fetters upon every unregenerate soul; there is abundant grace with God, there is utter destitution with themselves. Bound with such fetters, and led into the presence of Jesus, the captive would soon receive the liberty of the children of God.

I intend only to dwell this morning, or mainly, upon the first thought, the master thought, as it seems to me, which was in the prodigal's mind—that which really constrained him to say, "I will arise and go to my father." It was not, I think, the home-bringing thought that he was perishing with hunger, but the impulse towards his father found its mainspring in the consideration, "How many hired servants of my father's have bread enough and to spare!" The plenty, the abundance, the superabundance of the father's house, was that which attracted him to return home; and many, many a soul has been led to seek God when it has fully believed that there was abundant mercy with him. My desire this morning shall be to put plainly before every sinner here the exceeding abundance of the grace of God in Christ Jesus, hoping that the Lord will find out those who are his sons, and that they may catch at these words, and as they hear of the abundance of the bread in the Father's house, may say, "I will arise and go to my Father."

I. First, then, let us consider for a short time THE MORE THAN ABUNDANCE OF ALL GOOD THINGS IN THE FATHER'S HOUSE. What dost thou need this morning, awakened sinner? Of all that thou needest, there is with God an all-sufficient, a superabounding supply; "bread enough and to spare." Let us prove this to thee. First, *consider the Father himself*, and whosoever shall rightly consider the Father, will at once perceive that there can be no stint to mercy, no bound to the possibilities of grace. What is the nature and character of the Supreme? "Is he harsh or loving?" saith one. The Scripture answers the question, not by telling us that God is loving, but by assuring us that God is love. God himself is love; it is his very essence. It is not that love is in God, but that God himself is love. Can there be a more concise and more positive way of saying that the love of God is infinite? You cannot measure God himself; your conceptions cannot grasp the grandeur of his attributes, neither can you tell the dimensions of his love, nor conceive the fulness of it. Only this know, that high as the heavens are above the earth, so are his ways higher than your ways, and his thoughts than your thoughts. His mercy endureth for ever. He pardoneth iniquity, and passeth by the transgression of the remnant of his heritage. He retaineth not his anger for ever, because he delighteth in mercy. "Thou, Lord, art good, and ready to forgive: and plenteous in mercy unto all them that call upon thee." "Thy mercy is great above the heavens." "The Lord is very pitiful, and of tender mercy."

If divine love alone should not seem sufficient for your salvation, remember that with the Father to whom the sinner returns, there is as much of wisdom as there is of grace. Is thy case a very difficult one? He that made thee can heal thee. Are thy diseases strange and complex? He that fashioned the ear, can he not remove its deafness? He that made the eye, can he not enlighten it if it be blind? No mischief can have happened to thee, but what he who is thy God can recover thee from it. Matchless wisdom cannot fail to meet the intricacies of thy case.

Neither can there be any failure of power with the Father. Dost thou not know that he who made the earth, and stretched out the heavens like a tent to dwell in, hath no bound to his strength, nor limit to his might? If thou needest omnipotence to lift thee up from the slough into which thou hast fallen, omnipotence is ready to deliver thee, if thou cry to the strong for strength. Though thou shouldest need all the force with which the Creator made the worlds, and all the strength with which he bears up the pillars of the universe, all that strength and force should be laid out for thy good, if thou wouldst believingly seek mercy at the hand of God in Christ Jesus. None of his power shall be against thee, none of his wisdom shall plan thy overthrow; but love shall reign in all, and every attribute of God shall become subservient to thy salvation. Oh, when I think of sin I cannot understand how a sinner can be saved; but when I think of God, and look into his heart, I understand how readily he can forgive. "Look into his heart," saith one; "how can we do that?" Hath he not laid bare his heart to you? Do you enquire where he has done this? I answer, yonder, upon Calvary's cross. What was in the very centre of the divine heart? What, but the person of the Well-beloved, his only begotten Son? And he hath taken his only begotten and nailed him to the cross, because, if I may venture so to speak, he loved sinners better than his Son. He spared not his Son, but he spares the sinner; he poured out his wrath upon his Son and made him the substitute for sinners, that he might lavish love upon the guilty who deserved his anger. O soul, if thou art lost, it is not from any want of grace, or wisdom, or power in the Father; if thou perish, it is not because God is hard to move or unable to save. If thou be a castaway, it is not because the Eternal refused to hear thy cries for pardon or rejected thy faith in him. On thine own head be thy blood, if thy soul be lost. If thou starve, thou starvest because thou wilt starve; for in the Father's house there is "bread enough and to spare."

But, now, consider a second matter which may set this more clearly before us. Think of *the Son of God*, who is indeed the true bread of life for sinners. Sinner, I return to my personal address. Thou needest a Saviour; and thou mayst well be encouraged when thou seest that a Saviour is provided—provided by God, since it is certain he would not make a mistake in the provision. But consider who the Saviour is. He is himself God. Jesus who came from heaven for our redemption was not an angel, else might we tremble to trust the weight of our sin upon him. He was not mere man, or he could but have suffered as a substitute for one, if indeed for one; but he was very God of very God, in the beginning with the Father. And does such a one come to redeem? Is there room to doubt as to his ability, if that be the fact? I do confess this day, that if my sins were ten thousand times heavier than they are, yea, and if I had all the sins of this crowd in addition piled upon me, I could trust Jesus with them all at this moment now that I know him to be the Christ of God. He is the mighty God, and by his pierced hand the burden of our sins is easily removed; he blotteth out our sins, he casts them into the depths of the sea.

But think of what Jesus the Son of God has done. He who was God, and thus blessed for ever, left the throne and royalties of heaven, and stooped to yonder manger. There he lies; his mother wraps him in swaddling clothes, he hangs upon her breast; the Infinite is clothed as an infant, the Invisible is made manifest in flesh, the Almighty is linked with weakness, for our sakes. Oh, matchless stoop of condescension! If the Redeemer God does this in order to save us, shall it be thought a thing impossible for him to save the vilest of the vile? Can anything be too hard for him who comes from heaven to earth to redeem?

Pause not because of astonishment, but press onward. Do you see him who was God over all, blessed for ever, living more than thirty years in the midst of the sons of men, bearing the infirmities of manhood, taking upon himself our sicknesses, and sharing our sorrows: his feet weary with treading the acres of Palestine; his body faint oftentimes with hunger and thirst, and labour; his knees knit to the earth with midnight prayer; his eyes red with weeping (for ofttimes Jesus wept), tempted in all points like as we are? Matchless spectacle! An incarnate God dwells among sinners, and endures their contradiction! What glory flashed forth ever and anon from the midst of his lowliness! a glory which should render faith in him inevitable. Thou who didst walk the sea: thou who didst raise the dead, it is not rational to doubt thy power to forgive sins! Didst thou not thyself put it so when thou badest the man take up his bed and walk? "Whether is easier, to say, Thy sins be forgiven thee; or to say, Rise up and walk?" Assuredly he is able to save to the uttermost them that come unto God by him: he was able even here on earth in weakness to forgive sins, much more now that he is seated in his glory. He is exalted on high to be a Prince and a Saviour, to give repentance and remission of sins.

But, ah! the master proof that in Christ Jesus there is "bread enough and to spare," is the cross. Will you follow me a moment, will you follow him, rather, to Gethsemane? Can you see the bloody sweat as it falls upon the ground in his agony? Can you think of his scourging before Herod and Pilate? Can you trace him along the *Via Dolorosa* of Jerusalem? Will your tender hearts endure to see him nailed to the tree, and lifted up to bleed and die? This is but the shell; as for the inward kernel of his sufferings no language can describe it, neither can conception peer into it. The everlasting God laid sin on Christ, and where the sin was laid there fell the wrath. "It pleased the Lord to bruise him; he hath put him to grief." Now he that died upon the cross was God's only begotten Son. Can you conceive a limit to the merit of such a Saviour's death? I know there are some who think it necessary to their system of theology to limit the merit of the blood of Jesus: if my system of theology needed such a limitation, I would cast it to the winds. I cannot, dare not, allow the thought to find a lodging in my mind; it seems so near akin to blasphemy. In Christ's finished work I see an ocean of merit; my plummet finds no bottom, my eye discovers no shore. There must be sufficient efficacy in the blood of Christ, if God had so willed it, to have saved not only all this world, but ten thousand worlds, had they transgressed the Maker's law. Once admit infinity into the matter, and limit is out of the question. Having a divine person for an offering, it is not consistent to conceive of limited value; bound and measure are terms inapplicable to the divine sacrifice. The intent of the divine purpose fixes the application of the infinite offering, but does not change it into a finite work. In the atonement of Christ Jesus there is "bread enough and to spare;" even as Paul wrote to Timothy, "He is the Saviour of all men, specially of those that believe."

But now let me lead you to another point of solemnly joyful consideration, and that is *the Holy Spirit.* To believe and love the Trinity is to possess the key of theology. We spoke of the Father, we spoke of the Son; let us now speak of the Holy Spirit. We do him all too little honour, for the Holy Spirit condescends to come to earth and dwell in our hearts; and notwithstanding all our provocations he still abides within his people. Now, sinner, thou needest a new life and thou needest holiness, for both of these are necessary to make thee fit for heaven. Is there a provision for this? The Holy Spirit is provided and given in the covenant of grace; and surely in him there is "enough and to spare." What cannot the Holy Spirit do? Being divine, nothing can be beyond his power. Look at what he has already done. He moved upon the face of chaos, and brought it into order; all the beauty of creation arose beneath his moulding breath. We ourselves must confess with Elihu, "The Spirit of God hath made me, and the breath of the Almighty hath given me life." Think of the great deeds of the Holy Spirit at Pentecost, when men unlearned spake with tongues of which they knew not a syllable aforetime, and the flames of fire upon them were also within them, so that their hearts burned with zeal and courage to which they hitherto had been strangers. Think of the Holy Spirit's work on such a one as Saul of Tarsus. That persecutor foams blood, he is a very wolf, he would devour the saints of God at Damascus, and yet, within a few moments, you hear him say, "Who art thou, Lord?" and yet again, "Lord, what wilt thou have me to do?" His heart is changed; the Spirit of God has new created it; the adamant is melted in a moment into wax. Many of us stand before you as the living monuments of what the Holy Ghost can do, and we can assure you from our own experience, that there is no inward evil which he cannot overcome, no lustful desire of the flesh which he cannot subdue, no obduracy of the affections which he cannot melt. Is anything too hard for the Lord? Is the Spirit of the Lord straitened? Surely no sinner can be beyond the possibilities of mercy when the Holy Spirit condescends to be the agent of human conversion. O sinner, if thou perish, it is not because the Holy Spirit wants power, or the blood of Jesus lacks efficacy, or the Father fails in love; it is because thou believest not in Christ, but dost abide in wilful rebellion, refusing the abundant bread of life which is placed before thee.

A few rapid sentences upon other things, which will go to show still further the greatness of the provision of divine mercy. Observe well that *throughout all the ages God has been sending one prophet after another*, and these prophets have been succeeded by apostles, and these by martyrs and confessors, and pastors and evangelists, and teachers; all these have been commissioned by the Lord in regular succession; and what has been the message they have had to deliver? They have all pointed to Christ, the great deliverer. Moses and the prophets all spoke of him, and so have all truly God-sent ambassadors. Dost thou think, sinner, that God has made all this fuss about a trifle? Has he sent all these servants to call thee to a table insufficiently furnished? Has he multiplied his invitations through so long a time to bid thee and others come to a provision which is not, after all, sufficient for them? Oh, it cannot be! God is not mocked, neither does he mock poor needy souls. The stores of his mercy are sufficient for the utmost emergencies.

"Rivers of love and mercy here
In a rich ocean join;
Salvation in abundance flows,
Like floods of milk and wine.

Great God, the treasures of thy love
Are everlasting mines,
Deep as our helpless miseries are,
And boundless as our sins."

Recollect, again, that *God has been pleased to stake his honour upon the gospel.* Men desire a name, and God also is jealous of his glory. Now, what has God been pleased to select for his name? Is it not the conversion and salvation of men? When instead of the brier shall come up the myrtle-tree, and instead of the thorn shall come up the fir-tree, it shall be to the Lord for a name, for an everlasting sign that shall not be cut off. And dost thou think God will get a name by saving little sinners by a little Saviour? Ah! his great name comes from washing out stains as black as hell, and pardoning sinners who were foulest of the foul. Is there one monstrous rebel here who is qualified to glorify God greatly, because his salvation will be the wonder of angels and the amazement of devils? I hope there is. O thou most degraded, black, loathsome sinner, nearest to being a damned sinner, if this voice can reach thee, I challenge thee to come and prove whether God's mercy is not a match for thy sin. Thou Goliath sinner, come thou hither; thou shalt find that God can slay thine enmity, and make thee yet his friend, and the more his loving and adoring servant, because great forgiveness shall secure great love. Such is the greatness of divine mercy, that "where sin abounded, grace doth much more abound."

Dost thou think, again, O sinner, that Jesus Christ came out of heaven to do a little deed, and to provide a slender store of mercy? Dost thou think he went up to Calvary, and down to the grave, and all, that he might do a commonplace thing, and provide a stinted, narrow, limited salvation, such as thine unbelief would imagine his redemption to be? No. We speak of the labours of Hercules, but these were child's play compared with the labours of Christ who slew the lion of hell, turned a purifying stream through the Augean stables of man's sin, and cleansed them, and performed ten thousand miracles besides: and will you so depreciate Christ as to imagine that what he has accomplished is, after all, little, so little that it is not enough to save you? If it were in my power to single out the man who has been the most dishonest, most licentious, most drunken, most profane—in three words, most earthly, sensual, devilish—I would repeat the challenge which I gave just now, and bid him draw near to Jesus, and see whether the fountain filled with Christ's atoning blood cannot wash him white. I challenge him at this instant to come and cast himself at the dear Redeemer's feet, and see if he will say, "I cannot save thee, thou hast sinned beyond my power." It shall never, never, never be, for he is able to the uttermost to save. He is a Saviour, and a great one. Christ will be honoured by the grandeur of the grace which he bestows upon the greatest of offenders. There is in him pardon "enough and to spare."

I must leave this point, but I cannot do so without adding that I think "BREAD ENOUGH AND TO SPARE" might be taken for the motto of the gospel. I believe in particular redemption, and that Christ laid down his life for his sheep; but, as I have already said, I do not believe in the limited value of that redemption; how else could I dare to read the words of John, "He is the propitiation for our sins: and not for ours only, but also for the sins of the whole world." There is a sure portion for his own elect, but there is also over and above "to spare." I believe in the electing love which will save all its objects—"bread enough;" but I believe in boundless benevolence, "Bread enough *and to spare.*" We, when we have a purpose to accomplish, put forth the requisite quantity of strength and no more, for we must be economical, we must not waste our limited store; even charity gives the poor man no more than he absolutely needs; but when God feeds the multitude, he spreads the board with imperial bounty. Our water-cart runs up and down the favoured road, but when heaven's clouds would favour the good man's fields, they deluge whole nations, and even pour themselves upon the sea. There is no real waste with God; but at the same time there is no stint. "BREAD ENOUGH AND TO SPARE;" write that inscription over the house of mercy, and let every hungry passer-by be encouraged thereby to enter in and eat.

II. We must now pass on to a second consideration, and dwell very briefly on it. According to the text, there was not only bread enough in the house, but THE LOWEST IN THE FATHER'S HOUSE ENJOYED ENOUGH AND TO SPARE.

We can never make a parable run on all fours, therefore we cannot find the exact counterpart of the "hired servants." I understand the prodigal to have meant this, that the very lowest menial servant employed by his father had bread to eat, and had "bread enough and to spare." Now, how should we translate this? Why, sinner, the very lowest creature that God has made, that has not sinned against him, is well supplied and has abounding happiness. There are adaptations for pleasure in the organisations of the lowest animals. See how the gnats dance in the summer's sunbeam; hear the swallows as they scream with delight when on the wing. He who cares for birds and insects will surely care for men. God who hears the ravens when they cry, will he not hear the returning penitent? He gives these insects happiness; did he mean me to be wretched? Surely he who opens his hand and supplies the lack of every living thing, will not refuse to open his hand and supply my needs if I seek his face.

Yet I must not make these lowest creatures to be the hired servants. Whom shall I then select among men? I will put it thus. The very worst of sinners that have come to Christ have found grace "enough and to spare," and the very least of saints who dwell in the house of the Lord find love "enough and to spare." Take then *the most guilty of sinners*, and see how bountifully the Lord treats them when they turn unto him. Did not some of you, who are yourselves unconverted, once know persons who were at least as bad, perhaps more outwardly immoral than yourselves? Well, they have been converted, though you have not been; and when they were converted, what was their testimony? Did the blood of Christ avail to cleanse them? Oh, yes; and more than cleanse them, for it added to beauty not their own. They were naked once; was Jesus able to clothe them? Was there a sufficient covering in his righteousness? Ah, yes! and adornment was superadded; they received not a bare apparel, but a royal raiment. You have seen others thus liberally treated, does not this induce you also to come? Some of us need not confine our remarks to others, for we can speak personally of ourselves. We came to Jesus as full of sin as ever *you* can be, and felt ourselves beyond measure lost and ruined; but, oh, his tender love! I could sooner stand here and weep than speak to you of it. My soul melts in gratitude when I think of the infinite mercy of God to me in that hour when I came seeking mercy at his hands. Oh! why will not you also come? May his Holy Spirit sweetly draw you! I proved that there was bread enough, mercy enough, forgiveness enough, and to spare. Come along, come along, poor guilty one; come along, there is room enough for thee.

Now, if the chief of sinners bear this witness, so do *the most obscure of saints.* If we could call forth from his seat a weak believer in God, who is almost unknown in the church, one who sometimes questions whether he is indeed a child of God, and would be willing to be a hired servant so long as he might belong to God, and if I were to ask him, "Now after all how has the Lord dealt with you?" what would be his reply? You have many afflictions, doubts and fears, but have you any complaints against your Lord? When you have waited upon him for daily grace, has he denied you? When you have been full of troubles, has he refused you comfort? When you have been plunged in distress, has he declined to deliver you? The Lord himself asks, "Have I been a wilderness unto Israel?" Testify against the Lord, ye his people, if ye have aught against him. Hear, O heavens, and give ear, O earth, whosoever there be in God's service who has found him a hard task-master, let him speak. Amongst the angels before Jehovah's throne, and amongst men redeemed on earth, if there be any one that can say he hath been dealt with unjustly or treated with ungenerous churlishness, let him lift up his voice! But there is not one. Even the devil himself when he spoke of God and of his servant Job, said, "Doth Job serve God for nought?" Of course he did not: God will not let his servants serve him for nought; he will pay them superabundant wages, and they shall all bear witness that at his table there is "bread enough and to spare." Now, if these still enjoy the bread of the Father's house, these who were once great sinners, these who are now only very commonplace saints, surely, sinner, it should encourage you to say, "I will arise and go to my Father," for his hired servants "have bread enough and to spare."

III. Notice in the third place, that the text dwells upon THE MULTITUDE OF THOSE WHO HAVE "BREAD ENOUGH AND TO SPARE." The prodigal lays an emphasis upon that word, "*How many* hired servants of my father's!" He was thinking of their great number, and counting them over. He thought of those that tended the cattle, of those that went out with the camels, of those that watched the sheep, and those that minded the corn, and those that waited in the house; he ran them over in his mind: his father was great in the land, and had many servants; yet he knew that they all had of the best food "enough and to spare." "Why should I perish with hunger? I am only one at any rate; though my hunger seem insatiable, it is but one belly that has to be filled, and, lo, my father fills hundreds, thousands every day; why should I perish with hunger?" Now, O thou awakened sinner, thou who dost feel this morning thy sin and misery, think of the numbers upon whom God has bestowed his grace already. Think of the countless hosts in heaven: if thou wert introduced there to-day, thou wouldst find it as easy to tell the stars, or the sands of the sea, as to count the multitudes that are before the throne even now.

They have come from the east and from the west, and they are sitting down with Abraham, with Isaac, and with Jacob, and there is room enough for thee. And beside those in heaven, think of those on earth. Blessed be God, his elect on earth are to be counted by millions, I believe, and the days are coming, brighter days than these, when there shall be multitudes upon multitudes brought to know the Saviour, and to rejoice in him. The Father's love is not for a few only, but for an exceeding great company. A number that no man can number will be found in heaven; now, a man can number a very great amount. Set to work your Newtons, your calculators, they can count great numbers, but God and God alone can tell the multitude of his redeemed. Now, sinner, thou art but one at any rate, great sinner as thou art, and the mercy of God which embraces millions must have room enough in it for thee. The sea which holds the whales and creeping things innumerable, dost thou say, "It will overflow its banks if I bathe therein"? The sun which floods the universe with light, canst thou say, "I should exhaust his beams if I should ask him to enlighten my darkness"? Say not so. If thou comest to thyself thou wilt not tolerate such a thought, but thou wilt remember with hope the richness of the Father's grace, even though thine own poverty stare thee in the face.

Let us add a few words to close with, close grappling words to some of you to whom God has sent his message this morning, and whom he intends to save. O you who have been long hearers of the gospel, and who know it well in theory, but have felt none of the power of it in your hearts, let me now remind you where and what you are! You are perishing. As the Lord liveth, there is but a step between you and death; but a step, nay, but a breath between you and hell. Sinner, if at this moment thy heart should cease its beating, and there are a thousand causes that might produce that result ere the clock ticks again, thou wouldst be in the flames of divine wrath. Canst thou bear to be in such peril? If you were hanging over a rock by a slender thread which must soon break, and if you would then fall headlong down a terrible precipice, you would not sleep, but be full of alarm. May you have sense enough, wit enough, grace enough, to be alarmed until you escape from the wrath to come.

Recollect, however, that while you are perishing, you are perishing in sight of plenty; you are famishing where a table is abundantly spread; what is more, there are those whom you know now sitting at that table and feasting. What sad perversity for a man to persist in being starved in the midst of a banquet, where others are being satisfied with good things!

But I think I hear you say, "I fear I have no right to come to Jesus." I will ask you this: have you any right to say that till you have been denied? Did you ever try to go to Christ? Has he ever rejected you? If then you have never received a repulse, why do you wickedly imagine that he would repel you? Wickedly, I say, for it is an offence against the Christ who opened his heart upon the cross, to imagine that he could repel a penitent. Have you any right to say, "But I am not one of those for whom mercy is provided"? Who told you so? Have you climbed to heaven and read the secret records of God election? Has the Lord revealed a strange decree to you, and said,

"Go and despair, I will have no pity on you"? If you say that God has so spoken, I do not believe you. In this sacred book is recorded what God has said, here is the sure word of testimony, and in it I find it said of no humble seeker that God hath shut him out from his grace. Why hast thou a right to invent such a fiction in order to secure thine own damnation? Instead thereof, there is much in the word of God and elsewhere to encourage thee in coming to Christ. He has not repelled one sinner yet; that is good to begin with: it is not likely that he would, for since he died to save sinners, why should he reject them when they seek to be saved? You say, "I am afraid to come to Christ." Is that wise? I have heard of a poor navigator who had been converted, who had but little education, but who knew the grace of our Lord Jesus Christ, and when dying, very cheerfully and joyfully longed to depart. His wife said to him, "But, mon, ain't ye afeared to stand before the judge?" "Woman," said he, "why should I be afeared of a man as died for me?" Oh, why should you be afraid of Christ who died for sinners? The idea of being afraid of him should be banished by the fact that he shed his blood for the guilty. You have much reason to believe from the very fact that he died, that he will receive you. Besides, you have his word for it, for he saith, "Him that cometh to me I will in no wise cast out"—for no reason, and in no way, and on no occasion, and under no pretence, and for no motive. "I will not not cast him out," says the original. "Him that cometh to me I will in no wise cast out." You say it is too good to be true that there can be pardon for you: this is a foolish measuring of God's corn with your bushel, and because it seems too good a thing for you to receive, you fancy it is too good for God to bestow. Let the greatness of the good news be one reason for believing that the news is true, for it is so like God.

"Who is a pardoning God like thee?
Or who hath grace so rich and free?"

Because the gospel assures us that he forgives great sins through a great Saviour, it looks as if it were true, since he is so great a God.

What should be the result of all this with every sinner here at this time? I think this good news should arouse those who have almost gone to sleep through despair. The sailors have been pumping the vessel, the leaks are gaining, she is going down, the captain is persuaded she must be a wreck. Depressed by such evil tidings, the men refuse to work; and since the boats are all stove in and they cannot make a raft, they sit down in despair. Presently the captain has better news for them. "She will float," he says; "the wind is abating too, the pumps tell upon the water, the leak can be reached yet." See how they work; with what cheery courage they toil on, because there is hope! Soul, there is hope! *There is hope!* THERE IS HOPE! To the harlot, to the thief, to the drunkard.

"There is no hope," says Satan. Liar that thou art, get thee back to thy den; for thee there is no hope; but for fallen man, though he be in the mire of sin up to his very neck, though he be at the gates of death, while he lives there is hope. There is hope for hopeless souls in the Saviour.

In addition to arousing us this ought to elevate the sinner's thoughts. Some years ago, there was a crossing-sweeper in Dublin, with his broom, at the corner, and in all probability his highest thoughts were to keep the crossing clean, and look for the pence. One day, a lawyer put his hand upon his shoulder, and said to him, "My good fellow, do you know that you are heir to a fortune of ten thousand pounds a year?" "Do you mean it?" said he. "I do," he said. "I have just received the information; I am sure you are the man." He walked away, *and he forgot his broom.* Are you astonished? Why, who would not have forgotten a broom when suddenly made possessor of ten thousand a year? So, I pray that some poor sinners, who have been thinking of the pleasures of the world, when they hear that there is hope, and that there is heaven to be had, will forget the deceitful pleasures of sin, and follow after higher and better things.

Should it not also purify the mind? The prodigal, when he said, "I will arise and go to my father," became in a measure reformed from that very moment. How, say you? Why, he left the swine-trough: more, he left the wine cup, and he left the harlots. He did not go with the harlot on his arm, and the wine cup in his hand, and say, "I will take these with me, and go to my father." It could not be. These were all left, and though he had no goodness to bring, yet he did not try to keep his sins and come to Christ. I shall close with this remark, because it will act as a sort of *caveat*, and be a fit word to season the wide invitations of the free gospel. Some of you, I fear, will make mischief even out of the gospel, and will dare to take the cross and use it for a gibbet for your souls. If God is so merciful, you will go therefore and sin the more; and because grace is freely given, therefore you will continue in sin that grace may abound. If you do this, I would solemnly remind you I have no grace to preach to such as you. "Your damnation is just;" it is the word of inspiration, and the only one I know that is applicable to such as you are; but every needy, guilty soul that desires a Saviour is told to-day to believe in Jesus, that is, trust in the substitution and sacrifice of Christ, trust him to take your sin and blot it out; trust him to take your soul and save it. Trust Christ entirely, and you are forgiven this very moment; you are saved this very instant, and you may rejoice now in the fact that being justified by faith you have peace with God through Jesus Christ our Lord. O come ye, come ye, come ye; come and welcome; come ye now to the Redeemer's blood. Holy Spirit, compel them to come in, that the house of mercy may be filled. Amen, and Amen.

The New Park Street Pulpit.

CONFESSION OF SIN—A SERMON WITH SEVEN TEXTS.

A Sermon

DELIVERED ON SABBATH MORNING, JANUARY 18, 1857, BY THE

REV. C. H. SPURGEON,

AT THE MUSIC HALL, ROYAL SURREY GARDENS.

MY sermon this morning will have seven texts, and yet I pledge myself that there shall be but three different words in the whole of them; for it so happens that the seven texts are all alike, occurring in seven different portions of God's holy Word. I shall require, however, to use the whole of them to exemplify different cases; and I must request those of you who have brought your Bibles with you to refer to the texts as I shall mention them.

The subject of this morning's discourse will be this—CONFESSION OF SIN. We know that this is absolutely necessary to salvation. Unless there be a true and hearty confession of our sins to God, we have no promise that we shall find mercy through the blood of the Redeemer. "Whosoever confesseth his sins and forsaketh them shall find mercy." But there is no promise in the Bible to the man who will not confess his sins. Yet, as upon every point of Scripture there is a liability of being deceived, so more especially in the matter of confession of sin. There be many who make a confession, and a confession before God, who notwithstanding, receive no blessing, because their confession has not in it certain marks which are required by God to prove it genuine and sincere, and which demonstrate it to be the work of the Holy Spirit. My text this morning consists of three words, "I have sinned." And you will see how these words, in the lips of different men, indicate very different feelings. While one says, "I have sinned," and receives forgiveness; another we shall meet with says, "I have sinned," and goes his way to blacken himself with worse crimes than before, and dive into greater depths of sin than heretofore he had discovered.

The Hardened Sinner.

PHARAOH—"I have sinned."—*Exodus ix. 27.*

I. The first case I shall bring before you is that of the HARDENED SINNER, who, when under terror, says, "I have sinned." And you will find the text in the book of Exodus, the 9th chap. and 27th verse: "And Pharaoh sent, and called for Moses and Aaron, and said unto them, I have sinned this time: the Lord is righteous, and I and my people are wicked."

But why this confession from the lips of the haughty tyrant? He was not often wont to humble himself before Jehovah. Why doth the proud one bow himself? You will judge of the value of his confession when you hear the circumstances under which it was made. "And Moses stretched forth his rod toward heaven; and the Lord sent thunder and hail, and the fire ran along upon the ground; and the Lord rained hail upon the land of Egypt. So that there was hail, and fire mingled with the hail, very grievous, such as there was none like it in all the land of Egypt since it became a nation." "Now," says Pharaoh, whilst the thunder is rolling through the sky, while the lightning-flashes are setting the very ground on fire, and while the hail is descending in big lumps of ice, now, says he, "I have sinned." He is but a type and specimen of multitudes of the same class. How many a hardened rebel on shipboard, when the timbers are strained and creaking, when the mast is broken, and the ship is drifting before the gale, when the hungry waves are opening their mouths to swallow the ship up alive and quick as those that go into the pit —how many a hardened sailor has then bowed his knee, with tears in his eyes, and cried, "I have sinned!" But of what avail and of what value was his confession? The repentance that was born in the storm died in the calm; that repentance of his that was begotten amidst the thunder and the lightning, ceased so soon as all was hushed in quiet, and the man who was a pious mariner when on board ship, became the most wicked and abominable of sailors when he placed his foot on *terra firma*. How often, too, have we seen this in a storm of thunder and lightning? Many a man's cheek is blanched when he hears the thunder rolling; the tears start to his eyes, and he cries, "O God, I have sinned!" while the rafters of his house are shaking, and the very ground beneath him reeling at the voice of God which is full of majesty. But alas, for such a repentance! When the sun again shines, and the black clouds are withdrawn, sin comes again upon the man, and he becomes worse than before. How many of the same sort of confessions, too, have we seen in times of cholera, and fever, and pestilence! Then our churches have been crammed with hearers, who, because so many funerals have passed their doors, or so many have died in the street, could not refrain from going up to God's house to confess their sins. And under that visitation, when one, two, and three have been lying dead in the house, or next door, how many have thought they would really turn to God! But, alas! when the pestilence had done its work, conviction ceased; and when the bell had tolled the last time for a death caused by cholera, then their hearts ceased to beat with penitence, and their tears did flow no more.

Have I any such here this morning? I doubt not I have hardened persons who would scorn the very idea of religion, who would count me a cant and hypocrite if I should endeavour to press it home upon them, but who know right well that religion is true, and who feel it in their times of terror! If I have such here this morning, let me solemnly say to them, "Sirs, you have forgotten the feelings you had in your hours of alarm; but, remember, God has not forgotten the vows you then made." Sailor, you said if God would spare you to see the land again, you would be his servant; you are not so, you have lied against God, you have made him a false promise, for you have never kept the vow which your lips did utter. You said, on a bed of sickness, that if he would spare your life you would never again sin as you did before; but here you are, and this week's sins shall speak for themselves. You are no better than you were before your sickness. Couldst thou lie to thy fellow-man, and yet go unreproved? And thinkest thou that thou wilt lie against God, and yet go unpunished? No; the vow, however rashly made, is registered in heaven; and though it be a vow which man cannot perform, yet, as it is a vow which he has made himself, and made voluntarily too, he shall be punished for the non-keeping it; and God shall execute vengeance upon him at last, because he said he would turn from his ways, and then when the blow was removed he did it not. A great outcry has been raised of late against tickets-of-leave; I have no doubt there are some men here, who before high heaven stand in the same position as the ticket-of-leave men stand to our government. They were about to die, as they thought; they promised good behaviour if they might be spared, and they are here to-day on ticket-of-leave in this world: and how have they fulfilled their promise? Justice might raise the same outcry against them as they do against the burglars so constantly let loose upon us. The avenging angel might say, "O God, these men said, if they were spared they would be so much better; if anything they are worse. How have they violated their promise, and how have they brought down divine wrath upon their heads!" This is the first style of penitence; and it is a style I hope none of you will imitate, for it is utterly worthless. It is of no use for you to say, "I have sinned," merely under the influence of terror, and then to forget it afterwards.

The Double-minded Man.

BALAAM—"I have sinned."—*Numbers xxii.* 34.

II. Now for a second text. I beg to introduce to you another character—the *double-minded man*, who says, "I have sinned," and feels that he has, and feels it deeply too, but who is so worldly-minded that he "loves the wages of unrighteousness." The character I have chosen to illustrate this, is that of *Balaam*. Turn to the book of Numbers, the 22nd chap. and the 34th verse: "And Balaam said unto the angel of the Lord, I have sinned."

"I have sinned," said Balaam; but yet he went on with his sin afterwards. One of the strangest characters of the whole world is Balaam. I have often marvelled at that man; he seems really in another sense to have come up to the lines of Ralph Erskine—

"To good and evil equal bent,
And both a devil and a saint."

For he did seem to be so. At times no man could speak more eloquently and more truthfully, and at other times he exhibited the most mean and sordid covetuousness that could disgrace human nature. Think you see Balaam; he stands upon the brow of the hill, and there lie the multitudes of Israel at his feet; he is bidden to curse them, and he cries, "How shall I curse whom God hath not cursed?" And God opening his eyes, he begins to tell even about the coming of Christ, and he says, "I shall see him, but not now: I shall behold him, but not nigh." And then he winds up his oration by saying—"Let me die the death of the righteous, and let my last end be like his!" And ye will say of that man, he is a hopeful character. Wait till he has come off the brow of the hill, and ye will hear him give the most diabolical advice to the king of Moab which it was even possible for Satan himself to suggest. Said he to the king, "You cannot overthrow these people in battle, for God is with them; try and entice them from their God." And ye know how with wanton lusts they of Moab tried to entice the children of Israel from allegiance to Jehovah; so that this man seemed to have the voice of an angel at one time, and yet the very soul of a devil in his bowels. He was a terrible character; he was a man of two things, a man who went all the way with two things to a very great extent. I know the Scripture says, "No man can serve two masters." Now this is often misunderstood. Some read it, "No man can *serve two* masters." Yes he can; he can serve three or four. The way to read it is this: "No man can serve two *masters*." They cannot both be masters. He can serve two, but they cannot both be his master. A man can serve two who are not his masters, or twenty either; he may live for twenty different purposes, but he cannot live for more than one master purpose—there can only be one master purpose in his soul. But Balaam laboured to serve two; it was like the people of whom it was said, "They feared the Lord, and served other gods." Or like Rufus, who was a loaf of the same leaven; for you know our old king Rufus painted God on one side of his shield, and the devil on the other, and had underneath, the motto: "Ready for both; catch who can." There are many such, who are ready for both. They meet a minister, and how pious and holy they are; on the Sabbath they are the most respectable and upright people in the world, as you would think; indeed they effect a drawling in their speech, which they think to be eminently religious. But on a week day, if you want to find the greatest rogues and cheats, they are some of those men who are so sanctimonious in their piety. Now, rest assured, my hearers, that no confession of sin can be genuine, unless it be a whole hearted one. It is of no use for you to say, "I have sinned," and then keep on sinning. "I have sinned," say you, and it is a fair, fair face you show; but, alas! alas! for the sin you will go away and commit. Some men seem to be born with two characters. I remarked when in the library at Trinity College, Cambridge, a very fine statue of Lord Byron. The librarian said to me, "Stand here, sir." I looked, and I said, "What a fine intellectual countenance! What a grand genius he was!" "Come here," he said, "to the other side." "Ah! what a demon! There stands the man that could defy the deity." He seemed to have such a scowl and such a dreadful leer in his face; even as Milton would have painted Satan when he said—"Better to reign in hell than serve in heaven." I turned away and said to the librarian, "Do you think the artist designed this?" "Yes," he said, "he wished to picture the two characters—the great, the grand, the almost superhuman genius that he possessed, and yet the enormous mass of sin that was in his soul." There are some men here of the same sort. I dare say, like Balaam, they would overthrow everything in argument with their enchantments; they could work miracles; and yet at the same time there is something about them which betrays a horrid character of sin, as great as that which would appear to be their character for righteousness. Balaam, you know, offered sacrifices to God upon the altar of Baal: that was just the type of his character. So many do; they offer sacrifices to God on the shrine of Mammon; and whilst they will give to the building of a church, and distribute to the poor, they will at the other door of their counting-house grind the poor for bread, and press the very blood out of the widow, that they may enrich themselves. Ah! it is idle and useless for you to say, "I have sinned," unless you mean it from your heart. That double minded man's confession is of no avail.

The Insincere Man.

SAUL—"I have sinned."—1 *Samuel xv.* 24.

III. And now a third character, and a third text. In the first book of Samuel, the 15th chap. and 24th verse: "And *Saul* said unto Samuel, I have sinned"

Here is the *insincere man*—the man who is not like Balaam, to a certain extent sincere in two things; but the man who is just the opposite—who has no prominent point in his character at all, but is moulded everlastingly by the circumstances that are passing over his head. Such a man was *Saul.* Samuel reproved him, and he said, "I have sinned." But he did not mean what he said: for if you read the whole verse you will find him saying, "I have sinned: for I have transgressed the commandment of the Lord, and thy words; *because I feared the people*:" which was a lying excuse. Saul never feared anybody; he was always ready enough to do his own will—he was the despot. And just before he had pleaded another excuse, that he had saved the bullocks and lambs to offer to Jehovah, and therefore both excuses could not have been true. You remember, my friends, that the most prominent feature in the character of Saul was his insincerity. One day he fetched David from his bed, as he thought, to put him to death in his house. Another time he declares, "God forbid that I should do aught against thee, my son David." One day, because David saved his life, he said, "Thou art more righteous than I; I will do so no more." The day before he had gone out to fight against his own son-in-law, in order to slay him. Sometimes Saul was among the prophets, easily turned into a prophet, and then afterwards among the witches; sometimes in one place, and then another, and insincere in everything. How many such we have in every Christian assembly; men who are very easily moulded! Say what you please to them, they always agree with you. They have affectionate dispositions, very likely a tender conscience; but then the conscience is so remarkably tender, that when touched it seems to give, and you are afraid to probe deeper,—it heals as soon it is wounded. I think I used the very singular comparison once before, which I must use again: there are some men who seem to have india-rubber hearts. If you do but touch them, there is an impression made at once; but then it is of no use, it soon restores itself to its original character. You may press them whatever way you wish, they are so elastic you can always effect your purpose; but then they are not fixed in their character, and soon return to be what they were before. O sirs, too many of you have done the same; you have bowed your heads in church, and said, "We have erred and strayed from thy ways;" and you did not mean what you said. You have come to your minister; you have said, "I repent of my sins;" you did not then feel you were a sinner; you only said it to please him. And now you attend the house of God; no one more impressible than you; the tear will run down your cheek in a moment, but yet. notwithstanding all that, the tear is dried as quickly as it is brought forth, and you remain to all intents and purposes the same as you were before. To say, "I have sinned," in an unmeaning manner, is worse than worthless, for it is a mockery of God thus to confess with insincerity of heart.

I have been brief upon this character; for it seemed to touch upon that of Balaam; though any thinking man will at once see there was a real contrast between Saul and Balaam, even though there is an affinity between the two. Balaam was the great bad man, great in all he did; Saul was little in everything except in stature—little in his good and little in his vice; and he was too much of a fool to be desperately bad, though too wicked to be at any time good: while Balaam was great in both: the man who could at one time defy Jehovah, and yet at another time could say, "If Balak would give me his house full of silver and gold, I cannot go beyond the word cr the Lord my God, to do less or more."

The Doubtful Penitent.

ACHAN—"I have sinned."—*Joshua vii.* 20.

IV. And now I have to introduce to you a very interesting case; it is the case of the doubtful penitent, the case of *Achan*, in the book of Joshua, the 7th chap. and the 20th verse: "And Achan answered Joshua, indeed I have sinned."

You know that Achan stole some of the prey from the city of Jericho—that he was discovered by lot, and put to death. I have singled this case out as the representative of some whose characters are doubtful on their death beds; who do repent apparently, but of whom the most we can say is, that we hope their souls are saved at last, but indeed we cannot tell. Achan, you are aware, was stoned with stones, for defiling Israel. But I find in the Mishna, an old Jewish exposition of the Bible, these words, "Joshua said to Achan, the Lord shall trouble thee *this* day." And the note upon it is—"He said *this* day, implying that he was only to be troubled in this life, by being stoned to death, but that God would have mercy on his soul, seeing that he had made a full confession of his sin." And I, too, am inclined, from reading the chapter, to concur in the idea of my venerable and now glorified predecessor, Dr. Gill, in believing that Achan really was saved, although he was put to death for the crime, as an example. For you will observe how kindly Joshua spoke to him. He said, "My son, give, I pray thee, glory to the Lord God of Israel, and make confession unto him; and tell me now what thou hast done; hide it not from me." And you find Achan making a very full confession. He says, "Indeed I have sinned against the Lord God of Israel, and thus and thus have I done. When I saw among the spoils a goodly Babylonish garment, and two hundred shekels of silver, and a wedge of gold of fifty shekels weight, then I coveted them, and took them; and, behold, they are hid in the earth in the midst of my tent, and the silver under it." It seems so full a confession, that if I might be allowed to judge, I should say, "I hope to meet Achan the sinner, before the throne of God." But I find Matthew Henry has no such opinion; and many other expositors consider that as his body was destroyed, so was his soul. I have, therefore, selected his case, as being one of doubtful repentance. Ah! dear friends, it has been my lot to stand by many a death-bed, and to see many such a repentance as this; I have seen the man, when worn to a skeleton, sustained by pillows in his bed; and he has said, when I have talked to him of judgment to come, "Sir, I feel I have been guilty, but Christ is good; I trust in him." And I have said within myself, "I believe the man's soul is safe." But I have always come away with the melancholy reflection that I had no proof of it, beyond his own words; for it needs proof in acts and in future life, in order to sustain any firm conviction of a man's salvation. You know that great fact, that a physician once kept a record of a thousand persons who thought they were dying, and whom he thought were penitents; he wrote their names down in a book as those, who, if they had died, would go to heaven; they did not die, they lived; and he says that out of the whole thousand he had not three persons who turned out well afterwards, but they returned to their sins again, and were as bad as ever. Ah! dear friends, I hope none of you will have such a death-bed repentance as that; I hope your minister or your parents will not have to stand by your bedside, and then go away and say, "Poor fellow, I hope he is saved. But alas! death-bed repentances are such flimsy things; such poor, such trivial grounds of hope, that I am afraid, after all, his soul may be lost." Oh! to die with a full assurance; oh! to die with an abundant entrance, leaving a testimony behind that we have departed this life in peace! That is a far happier way than to die in a doubtful manner, lying sick, hovering between two worlds, and neither ourselves nor yet our friends knowing to which of the two worlds we are going. May God grant us grace to give in our lives evidences of true conversion, that our case may not be doubtful!

The Repentance of Despair.

JUDAS—"I have sinned."—*Matthew xxvii.* 4.

V. I shall not detain you too long, I trust, but I must now give you another bad case; the worst of all. It is the REPENTANCE OF DESPAIR. Will you turn to the 27th chap. of Matthew, and the 4th verse? There you have a dreadful case of the repentance of despair You will recognize the character the moment I read the verse: "And Judas said, I have sinned." Yes, Judas the traitor, who had betrayed his Master, when he saw that his Master was condemned, "repented, and brought again the thirty pieces of silver to the chief priests and elders, saying, I have sinned, in that I have betrayed innocent blood, and cast down the pieces in the temple, and went" and what?—"and *hanged himself.*" Here is the worst kind of repentance of all; in fact, I know not that I am justified in calling it repentance; it must be called remorse of conscience. But Judas did confess his sin, and then went and hanged himself. Oh! that dreadful, that terrible, that hideous confession of despair. Have you never seen it? If you never have, then bless God that you never were called to see such a sight. I have seen it once in my life, I pray God I may never see it again,—the repentance of the man who sees death staring him in the face, and who says, "I have sinned." You tell him that Christ has died for sinners; and he answers, "There is no hope for me; I have cursed God to his face; I have defied him; my day of grace I know is past; my conscience is seared with a hot iron; I am dying, and I know I shall be lost!" Such a case as that happened long ago, you know, and is on record—the case of Francis Spira—the most dreadful case, perhaps, except that of Judas, which is upon record in the memory of man. Oh! my hearers, will any of you have such a repentance? If you do, it will be a beacon to all persons who sin in future; if you have such a repentance as that, it will be a warning to generations yet to come. In the life of Benjamin Keach—and he also was one of my predecessors—I find the case of a man who had been a professor of religion, but had departed from the profession, and had gone into awful sin. When he came to die, Keach, with many other friends, went to see him, but they could never stay with him above five minutes at a time; for he said, "Get ye gone; it is of no use your coming to me; I have sinned away the Holy Ghost; I am like Esau, I have sold my birthright, and though I seek it carefully with tears, I can never find it again." And then he would repeat dreadful words, like these: "My mouth is filled with gravel stones, and I drink wormwood day and night. Tell me not tell me not of Christ! I know he is a Saviour, but I hate him and he hates me. I know I must die; I know I must perish!" And then followed doleful cries, and hideous noises, such as none could bear. They returned again in his placid moments only to stir him up once more, and make him cry out in his despair, "I am lost! I am lost! It is of no use your telling me anything about it!" Ah! there may be a man here who may have such a death as that; let me warn him, ere he come to it; and may God the Holy Spirit grant that that man may be turned unto God, and made a true penitent, and then he need not have any more fear; for he who has had his sins washed away in a Saviour's blood, need not have any remorse for his sins, for they are pardoned through the Redeemer.

The Repentance of the Saint.

JOB.—"I have sinned."—*Job vii.* 20

VI. And now I come into daylight. I have been taking you through dark and dreary confessions; I shall detain you there no longer, but bring you out to the two good confessions which I have to read to you. The first is that of Job in 7th chap., at the 20th verse: "I have sinned; what shall I do unto thee, O thou preserver of men?" This is the *repentance of the saint.* Job was a saint, but he sinned. This is the repentance of the man who is a child of God already, an acceptable repentance before God. But as I intend to dwell upon this in the evening, I shall now leave it, for fear of wearying you. David was a specimen of this kind of repentance, and I would have you carefully study his penitential psalms, the language of which is ever full of weeping humility and earnest penitence.

The Blessed Confession.

THE PRODIGAL.—"I have sinned."—*Luke xv.* 18.

VII. I come now to the last instance, which I shall mention, it is the case of the prodigal. In Luke xv. 18, we find the prodigal says: "Father I have sinned." Oh, here is *a blessed confession!* Here is that which proves a man to be a regenerate character—"Father, I have sinned." Let me picture the scene. There is the prodigal; he has run away from a good home and a kind father, and he has spent all his money with harlots, and now he has none left. He goes to his old companions, and asks them for relief. They laugh him to scorn. "Oh," says he, "you have drunk my wine many a day; I have always stood paymaster to you in all our revelries; will you not help me?" "Get you gone" they say; and he is turned out of doors. He goes to all his friends with whom he had associated, but no man gives him anything. At last a certain citizen of the country said,—"You want something to do, do you? Well go and feed my swine." The poor prodigal, the son of a rich landowner, who had a great fortune of his own, has to go out to feed swine; and he a Jew too!—the worst employment (to his mind,) to which he could be put. See him there, in squalid rags, feeding swine; and what are his wages? Why, so little, that he "would fain have filled his belly with the husks the swine eat, but no man gave to him." Look, there he is, with the fellow commoners of the sty, in all his mire and filthiness. Suddenly a thought put there by the good Spirit, strikes his mind. "How is it," says he, "that in my father's house there is bread enough and to spare, and I perish with hunger? I will arise and go to my father, and will say unto him, Father, I have sinned against heaven and before thee, and am no more worthy to be called thy son: make me as one of thy hired servants." Off he goes. He begs his way from town to town. Sometimes he gets a lift on a coach, perhaps, but at other times he goes trudging his way up barren hills and down desolate vales, all alone. And now at last he comes to the hill outside the village, and sees his father's house down below. There it is; the old poplar tree against it, and there are the stacks round which he and his brother used to run and play; and at the sight of the old homestead all the feelings and associations of his former life rush upon him, and tears run down his cheeks, and he is almost ready to run away again. He says "I wonder whether father's dead I daresay mother broke her heart when I went away; I always was her favorite. And if they are either of them alive, they will never see me again; they will shut the door in my face. What am I to do? I cannot go back, I am afraid to go forward." And while he was thus deliberating, his father had been walking on the housetop, looking out for his son; and though he could not see his father, his father could see him. Well, the father comes down stairs with all his might, runs up to him, and whilst he is thinking of running away, his father's arms are round his neck, and he falls-to kissing him, like a loving father indeed, and then the son begins,—"Father, I have sinned against heaven and in thy sight, and am no more worthy to be called thy son," and he was going to say, "Make me as one of thy hired servants." But his father puts his hand on his mouth. "No more of that," says he; "I forgive you all; you shall not say anything about being a hired servant—I will have none of that. Come along," says he, "come in, poor prodigal. Ho!" says he to the servants, "bring hither the best robe, and put it on him, and put shoes on his poor bleeding feet; and bring hither the fatted calf and kill it; and let us eat and be merry: For this my son was dead, and is alive again; he was lost and is found. And they began to be merry." Oh, what a precious reception for one of the chief of sinners! Good Matthew Henry says—"His father saw him, there were eyes of mercy; he ran to meet him, there were legs of mercy; he put his arms round his neck, there were arms of mercy; he kissed him, there were kisses of mercy; he said to him—there were words of mercy,—Bring hither the best robe, there were deeds of mercy, wonders of mercy—all mercy. Oh, what a God of mercy he is."

Now, prodigal, you do the same. Has God put it into your heart? There are many who have been running away a long time now. Does God say "return?" Oh, I bid you return, then, for as surely as ever thou dost return he will take thee in. There never was a poor sinner yet who came to Christ, whom Christ turned away. If he turns you away, you will be the first. Oh, if you could but try him! "Ah, sir, I am so black, so filthy, so vile." Well come along with you—you cannot be blacker than the prodigal. Come to your Father's house, and as surely as he is God he will keep his word—"Him that cometh unto me I will in no wise cast out."

Oh, if I might hear that some had come to Christ this morning, I would indeed bless God! I must tell here for the honor of God and Christ, one remarkable circumstance, and then I have done. You will remember that one morning I mentioned the case of an infidel who had been a scorner and scoffer, but who, through reading one of my printed sermons, had been brought to God's house and then to God's feet. Well, last Christmas day, the same infidel gathered together all his books, and went into the market-place at Norwich, and there made a public recantation of all his errors, and a profession of Christ, and then taking up all his books which he had written, and had in his house, on evil subjects, burned them in the sight of the people. I have blessed God for such a wonder of grace as that, and pray that there may be many more such, who, though they be born prodigal, will yet return home, saying, "I have sinned."

The New Park Street Pulpit.

THE PRODIGAL'S RETURN.

A Sermon

DELIVERED ON SABBATH MORNING, FEBRUARY 7, 1858, BY THE

REV. C. H. SPURGEON,

AT THE MUSIC HALL, ROYAL SURREY GARDENS.

"But when he was yet a great way off, his father saw him, and had compassion, and ran, and fell on his neck, and kissed him."—Luke xv. 20.

ALL persons engaged in education will tell you that they find it far more difficult to make the mind unlearn its errors than to make it receive truth. If we could suppose a man totally ignorant of anything, we should have a fairer chance of instructing him quickly and effectually than we should have had if his mind had been previously stored with falsehood. I have no doubt you, each of you, find it harder to unlearn than to learn. To get rid of old prejudices and preconceived notions is a very hard struggle indeed. It has been well said, that those few words, "I am mistaken," are the hardest in all the English language to pronounce, and certainly it takes very much force to compel us to pronounce them: and after having done so, it is even then difficult to wipe away the slime which an old serpentine error has left upon the heart. Better for us not to have known at all than to have known the wrong thing. Now, I am sure that this truth is never more true than when it applies to God. If I had been let alone to form my notion of God, entirely from Holy Scripture, I feel, that with the assistance of his Holy Spirit, it would have been far more easy for me to understand what he is, and how he governs the world, than to learn even the truths of his own Word, after the mind had become perverted by the opinions of others. Why, brethren, who is it that gives a fair representation of God? The Arminian slanders God by accusing him (not in his own intention, but really so) of unfaithfulness; for he teaches that God may promise what he never performs; that he may give eternal life, and promise that those who have it shall never perish, and yet they may perish after all. He speaks of God as if he was a mutable being, for he talks of his loving men one day, and hating them the next; of his writing their names in the Book of Life one hour, and then erasing their names in the next. And the influence of such an error as that, is very baneful. Many children of God, who have imbibed these errors in early youth, have had to drag along their poor wearied and broken frames for many a day, whereas they might have walked joyfully to heaven if they had known the truth from the beginning. On the other hand, those who hear the Calvinistic preacher, are very apt to misinterpret God. Although we trust we would never speak of God in any other sense than that in which we find him represented in sacred Scripture, yet are we well aware that many of our hearers, even through our assertions, when most guarded, are apt to get rather a caricature of God, than a true picture of him. They imagine that God is a severe being, angry and fierce, very easily to be moved to wrath, but not so easily to be induced to love; they are apt to think of him as one who sits in supreme and lofty state, either totally indifferent to the wishes of his creatures, or else determined to have his own way with them, as an arbitrary Sovereign, never listening to their desires, or compassionating their woes. Oh that we could unlearn all these fallacies, and believe God to be what he is! Oh that we could come to Scripture, and there look into that glass which reflects his sacred image, and then receive him as he is, the all-Wise, the all-Just, and yet the all-Gracious, and all-Loving Jehovah! I shall endeavour this morning, by the help of God's Holy Spirit, to represent the lovely character of Christ; and if I shall be happy enough to have some in my audience who are in the position of the prodigal son in the parable—coming to Christ, and yet a great way off from him—I shall trust that they will be led by the same Divine Spirit, to believe in the lovingkindness of Jehovah, and so may find peace with God now, ere they leave this house of prayer.

"When he was yet a great way off, his father saw him, and had compassion, and ran, and fell on his neck, and kissed him." First, I shall notice the *position* intended in the words, "a great way off;" secondly, I shall notice the *peculiar troubles* which agitate the minds of those, who are in this condition; and then, thirdly, I shall endeavour to teach *the great lovingkindness of our own adorable God*, inasmuch as when we are "a great way off," he runs to us, and embraces us in the arms of his love.

I. First, then, what is the POSITION signified by being "a great way off?" I must just notice what is *not* that position. It is not the position of the man who is careless and entirely regardless of God; for you notice that the prodigal is represented now as having come to himself, and as returning to his father's house. Though it be true that all sinners are a great way off from God, whether they know it or not, yet in this particular instance, the position of the poor prodigal is intended to signify the character of one, who has been aroused by conviction, who has been led to abhor his former life, and who sincerely desires to return to God. I shall not, then, this morning, specially address the blasphemer, and the profane. To him, there may be some incidental warning heard, but I shall not specially address such a character. It is another person for whom this text is intended: the man who has been a blasphemer, if you please, who may have been a drunkard, and a swearer, and what not, but who has now renounced these things, and is steadfastly seeking after Christ, that he may obtain eternal life. That is the man who is here said to be, though coming to the Lord, "a great way off."

Once again, there is another person who is not intended by this description, namely, the very great man, the Pharisee who thinks himself extremely righteous, and has never learned to confess his sin. You, sir, in your apprehension, are not a great way off. You are so really in the sight of God; you are as far from him as light from darkness, as the east is from the west; but you are not spoken of here. You are like the prodigal son, only that instead of spending your life righteously, you have run away from your Father, and hidden in the earth the gold which he gave you, and are able to feed upon the husks which swine do eat, whilst by a miserable economy of good works you are hoping to save enough of your fortune to support yourself here and in eternity. Your hope of self-salvation is a fallacy, and you are not addressed in the words of the text. It is the man who knows himself lost, but desires to be saved, who is here declared to be met by God, and received with affectionate embraces.

And now we come to the question, Who is the man, and why is he said to be a great way off? For he seems to be very near the kingdom, now that he knows his need and is seeking the Saviour. I reply, in the first place, he is a great way off in his own apprehensions. You are here this morning, and you have an idea that never was man so far from God as you are. You look back upon your past life, and you recollect how you have slighted God, despised his Sabbath, neglected his Book, trampled upon the blood of sprinkling, and rejected all the invitations of his mercy. You turn over the pages of your history, and you remember the sins which you have committed—the sins of your youth and your former transgressions, the crimes of your manhood, and the riper sins of your older years. like black waves dashing upon a dark shore, they roll in wave upon wave, upon your poor troubled memory. There comes a little wave of your childish folly, and over that there leaps one of your youthful transgressions, and over the head of this there comes a very Atlantic billow of your manhood's transgressions. At the sight of them you stand astonished and amazed. "O Lord my God, how deep is the gulf which divides me from thyself, and where is the power that can bridge it? I am separated from thee by leagues of sin, whole mountains of my guilt are piled upwards between me and thyself. O God, shouldest thou destroy me now, thou wouldest be just; and if thou dost ever bring me to thyself, it must be nothing less than a power as Omnipotent as that which made the world, which can ever do it.

Oh! how far am I from God!" Some of you would be startled this morning, if your neighbours were to give you revelations of their own feelings. If yonder man standing there in the crowd could come into this pulpit, and tell out what he now feels, you might perhaps be horrified at his description of his own heart. How many of you have no notion of the way in which a soul is cut and hacked about, when it is under the convictions of the law! If you should hear the man tell out what he feels, you would say, "Ah! he is a poor deluded enthusiast; men are not so bad as that;" or else you would be apt to think he had committed some nameless crime which he dare not mention, that was preying on his conscience. Nay, sir, he has been as moral and as upright as you have been; but should he describe himself as he now discovers himself to be, he would shock you utterly. And yet you are the same, though you feel it not, and would indignantly deny it. When the light of God's grace comes into your heart, it is something like the opening of the windows of an old cellar that has been shut up for many days. Down in that cellar, which has not been opened for many months, are all kinds of loathsome creatures, and a few sickly plants blanched by the darkness. The walls are dark and damp with the trail of reptiles; it is a horrid filthy place in which no one would willingly enter. You may walk there in the dark very securely, and except now and then for the touch of some slimy creature, you would not believe the place was so bad and filthy. Open those shutters, clean a pane of glass, let a little light in, and now see how a thousand noxious things have made this place their habitation. Sure, 'twas not the light that made this place so horrible, but it was the light that showed how horrible it was before. So let God's grace just open a window and let the light into a man's soul, and he will stand astonished to see at what a distance he is from God. Yes, sir, to-day you think yourself second to none but the Eternal; you fancy that you can approach his throne with steady step; it is but a little that you have to do to be saved; you imagine that you can accomplish it at any hour, and save yourself upon your dying bed as well as now. Ah! sir, if you could but be touched by Ithuriel's wand, and made to be in appearance what you are in reality, then you would see that you are far enough from God even now, and so far from him, that unless the arms of his grace were stretched out to bring you to himself, you must perish in your sin. Now I turn my eye again with hope, and trust I have not a few in this large assembly, who can say, "Sir, I feel I am far from God, and sometimes I fear I am so far from him, that he will never have mercy upon me; I dare not lift so much as my eyes towards heaven; I smite on my breast, and say, 'Lord have mercy upon me, a sinner.'" Oh! poor heart; here is a comforting passage for thee: "When he was yet a great way off, his father saw him, and had compassion on him."

But again, there is a second sense in which some now present feel themselves to be far off from God. Conscience tells every man that if he would be saved he must get rid of his sin. The Antinomian may possibly pretend to believe that men can be saved while they live in sin; but conscience will never allow any man to swallow so egregious a lie as that. I have not one person in this congregation who is not perfectly assured that if he is to be saved he must leave off his drunkenness and his vices. Sure there is not one here so stupified with the laudanum of hellish indifference as to imagine that he can revel in his lusts, and afterwards wear the white robe of the redeemed in Paradise. If ye imagine ye can be partakers of the blood of Christ, and yet drink the cup of Belial; if ye imagine that ye can be members of Satan and members of Christ at the same time, ye have less sense than one would give you credit for. No, you know that right arms must be cut off, and right eyes plucked out—that the most darling sins must be renounced, if ye would enter into the kingdom of God. And I have a man here who is convinced of the unholiness of his life, and he has striven to reform, not because he thinks reformation would save him, for he knows better than that, but because he knows that this is one of the first fruits of grace—reformation from sin. Well, poor man, he has for many years been an inveterate drunkard, and he struggles now to overcome the passion. He has almost effected it; but he never had such an Herculean labour to attempt before; for now some temptation comes upon him so strongly, that it is as much as he can do to stand against it; and perhaps sometimes since his first conviction of sin he has even fallen into it. Or perhaps it is another vice, and you, my brother, have set your face against it; but there are many bonds and fetters that bind us to our vices, and you find that though it was easy enough to spin the warp and woof of sin together; it is not so easy to unravel that which you have spun. You cannot purge your house of your idols; you do not yet know how to give up all your lustful pleasures. Not yet can you renounce the company of the ungodly. You have cut off one by one your most intimate acquaintances, but it is very hard to do it completely, and you are struggling to accomplish it, and you often fall on your knees and cry, "O Lord, how far I am from thee! what high steps these are which I have to climb! Oh! how can I be saved? Sure, if I cannot purge myself from my old sins, I shall never be able to hold on my way; and even should I get rid of them, I should plunge into them once more." You are crying out, "Oh, how great my distance from God! Lord, bring me near!"

Let me present you with one other aspect of our distance from God. You have read your Bibles, and you believe that faith alone can unite the soul to Christ. You feel that unless you can believe in him who died upon the cross for your sins, you can never see the kingdom of God; but you can say this morning, "Sir, I have striven to believe; I have searched the Scriptures, not hours, but days together, to find a promise upon which my weary foot might rest; I have been upon my knees many and many a time, earnestly supplicating a divine blessing; but though I have pleaded, all in vain have I urged my plea, for until now no whisper have I had of grace, no token for good, no sign of mercy. Sir, I have striven to believe, and I have said,

'O could I but believe!
  Then all would easy be;
I would, but cannot—Lord, relieve,
  My help must come from thee!'

I have used all the power I have, and have desperately striven to cast myself at the Saviour's feet and see my sins washed away in his blood. I have not been indifferent to the story of the cross; I have read it a hundred times, and even wept over it; but when I strive to put my hand upon the scape-goat's head, and labour to believe that my sins are transferred to him, some demon seems to stop the breath that would breathe itself forth in adoration, and something checks the hand that would lay itself upon the head that died for me." Well, poor soul, thou art indeed far from God. I will repeat the words of the text to thee. May the Holy Spirit repeat them in thine ear! "When he was yet a great way off, his father saw him, and had compassion, and ran, and fell on his neck, and kissed him." So shall it be with thee if thou hast come thus far, though great may be the distance, thy feet shall not have to travel it, but God the Eternal One shall from his throne look down and visit thy poor heart, though now thou tarriest by the way afraid to approach him.

II. Our second point is the PECULIAR TROUBLES which agitate the breasts of those who are in this position. Let us introduce to you the poor ragged prodigal. After a life of ease, he is by his own vice plunged into penury and labour. After feeding swine for a time, and being almost starved, he sets about returning to his father's house. It is a long and weary journey. He walks many a mile until his feet are sore, and at last from the summit of a mountain he views his father's house far away in the plain. There are yet many miles between him and his father whom he has neglected. Can you conceive his emotions when for the first time after so long an absence he sees the old house at home? He remembers it well in the distance; for though it is long since he trod its floors he has never ceased to recollect it; and the remembrance of his father's kindness, and of his own prosperity when he was with him, has never yet been erased from his consciousness. You would imagine that for one moment he feels a flash of joy, like some flash of lightning in the midst of the tempest, but anon a black darkness comes over his spirit. In the first place, it is probable he will think, "Oh! suppose I could reach my home, will my father receive me? Will he not shut the door in my face and tell me to begone and spend the rest of my life where I have been spending the first of it?" Then another suggestion might arise: "Surely, the demon that led me first astray may lead me back again, before I salute my parent." "Or mayhap," thought he, "I may even die upon the road, and so before I have received my father's blessing my soul may stand before its God." I doubt not each of these three thoughts has crossed your mind if you are now in the position of one who is seeking Christ, but mourns to feel himself far away from him.

First, you have been afraid lest you should die before Christ has appeared to you. You have been for months seeking the Saviour without finding him, and now the black thought comes, "And what if I should die with all these prayers unanswered? Oh! if he would but hear me ere I departed this world I would be content, though he should keep me waiting in anguish for many years. But what, if before to-morrow morning I should be a corpse? At my bed I kneel to-night and cry for mercy. Oh! if he should not send the pardon before to-morrow morning, and in the night my spirit should stand before his bar!—What then?" It is singular that other men think they shall live for ever, but men convinced of sin, who seek a Saviour, are afraid they shall not live another moment. You have known the time, dear Christian brethren, when you dared not shut your eyes for fear you should not open them again on earth; when you dreaded the shadows of the night lest they should darken for ever the light of the sun, and you should dwell in outer darkness throughout eternity. You have mourned as each day has entered, and you have wept as it has departed, because you fancied that your next step might precipitate you into your eternal doom. I have known what it is to tread the earth and fear lest every tuft of grass should but cover a door to hell; trembling, lest every particle, and every atom, and every stone, should be so at league with God against me, as to destroy me. John Bunyan says, that at one time in his experience, he felt that he had rather have been born a dog or a toad than a man; he felt so unutterably wretched on account of sin; and his great point of wretchedness was the fact, that though he had been three years seeking Christ, he might after all die without finding him. And in truth, this is no needless alarm. It may be perhaps too alarming to some who already feel their need of Christ, but the mass of us need perpetually to be startled with the thought of death. How few of you ever indulge that thought! Because ye live and are in health, and eat, and drink, and sleep, ye think ye shall not die. Do ye ever soberly look at your last end? Do ye ever, when ye come to your beds at night, think how one day ye shall undress for the last slumber? And when ye wake in the morning, do ye never think that the trump of the archangel shall startle you to appear before God in the last day of the great assize, wherein an universe shall stand before the Judge? No. "All men think all men mortal but themselves;" and thoughts of death we still push off, until at last we shall find ourselves waking up in torment, where to wake is to wake too late. But thou to whom I specially speak this morning, thou who feelest that thou art a great way off from Christ, thou shalt never die, but live, and declare the works of the Lord; if thou hast really sought him, thou shalt never die until thou hast found him. There was never a soul yet, that sincerely sought the Saviour, who perished before he found him. No; the gates of death shall never shut on thee till the gates of grace have opened for thee; till Christ has washed thy sins away thou shalt never be baptized in Jordan's flood. Thy life is secure, for this is God's constant plan—he keeps his own elect alive till the day of his grace, and then he takes them to himself. And inasmuch as thou knowest thy need of a Saviour, thou art one of his, and thou shalt never die until thou hast found him.

Your second fear is, "Ah, sir! I am not afraid of dying before I find Christ, I have a worse fear than that; I have had convictions before, and they have often passed away; my greatest fear to-day is, that these will be the same." I have heard of a poor collier, who on one occasion, having been deeply impressed under a sermon, was led to repent of sin and forsake his former life; but he felt so great a horror of ever returning to his former conversation, that one day he knelt down and cried thus unto God, "O Lord, let me die on this spot, rather than ever deny the religion which I have espoused, and turn back to my former conversation:" and we are credibly told, that he died on that very spot, and so his prayer was answered. God had rather take him home to heaven than suffer him to bear the brunt of temptation on earth. Now, when men come to Christ, they feel that they had rather suffer anything than lose their convictions. Scores of times have you and I been drawn to Christ under the preaching of the Word. We can look back upon dozens of occasions on which it seemed just the turning point with us. Something said in our hearts, "Now, believe in Christ, now is the accepted time, now is the day of salvation." But we said, "To-morrow, to-morrow;" and when to-morrow came our convictions were gone. We thought what we said yesterday would be the deed of to-day; but instead of it, the procrastination of yesterday became the hardened wickedness of to-day: we wandered farther from God and forgot him. Now you are crying to him for fear, lest he should give you up again. You have this morning prayed before you came here, and you said, "Father, suffer not my companions to laugh me out of my religion; let not my worldly business so engross my thoughts, as to prevent my due attention to the matters of another world. Oh, let not the trifles of to-day so absorb my thoughts that I may not be preparing myself to meet my God—

'Deeply on my thoughtful heart,
Eternal things impress,'

and make this a real saving work that shall never die out, nor be taken from me.' Is that your earnest prayer? O poor prodigal, it shall be heard, it shall be answered. Thou shalt not have time to go back. To-day thy Father views thee from his throne in heaven; to-day he runs to thee in the message of his gospel; to-day he falls upon thy neck and weeps for joy; to-day he says to thee, "Thy sins, which are many, are all forgiven;" to-day, by the preaching of the Word, he bids thee come and reason with him, "for though thy sins be as scarlet, they shall be as wool, though they be red like crimson, they shall be whiter than snow."

But the last and the most prominent thought which I suppose the prodigal would have, would be, that when he did get to his father, he would say to him, "Get along with you, I will have nothing more to do with you." "Ah!" thought he to himself, "I recollect the morning when I rose up before day-break, because I knew I could not stand my mother's tears; I remember how I crept down the back staircase and took all the money with me, how I stole down the yard and ran away into the land where I spent my all. Oh! what will the old gentleman say of me when I come back? Why, there he is! He is running to me. But he has got a horsewhip with him, to be sure, to whip me away. It is not at all possible that if he comes he will have a kind word for me. The most I can expect is that he will say, 'Well John, you have wasted all your money, you cannot expect me to do anything for you again. I won't let you starve; you shall be one of my servants; there, come, I will take you as footman;' and if he will do that I will be obliged to him; nay, that is the very thing I will ask of him; I will say, 'Make me as one of thy hired servants.'" "Oh," said the devil within him, "your father will never speak comfortably to you: you had better run away again. I tell you if he gets near you, you will have such a dressing as you never received in your life. You will die with a broken heart; you will very likely fall dead here; the old man will never bury you; the carrion crows will eat you. There is no hope for you: see how you have treated him. Put yourself in his place: what would you do if you had a son that had run away with half your living, and spent it upon harlots?" And the son thought if he were in his father's place he should be very harsh and severe; and possibly, he almost turned upon his heel to run away. But he had not time to do that. When he was just thinking about running away, on a sudden his father's arms were about his neck, and he had received the paternal kiss. Nay, before he could get his whole prayer finished, he was arrayed in a white robe, the best in the house; and they had brought him to the table, and the fatted calf was being killed for his repast. And poor soul, it shall be so with you. Thou sayest, "If I go to God, he will never receive me. I am too vile and wretched: others he may have pressed to his heart, but he will not me. If my brother should go, he might be saved; but there are such aggravations in my crime; I have grown so old since; I have done such a deal of mischief; I have so often blasphemed him, so frequently broken his Sabbaths; ah! and I have so often deceived him; I have promised I would repent, and when I have got well I have lied to God, and gone back to my old sin. Oh, if he would but let me creep inside the door of heaven! I will not ask to be one of his children; I will only ask that he will let me be where the Syro-Phœnician woman desired to be—to be a dog, to eat the crumbs that fall from the Master's table. That is all I ask; and oh! if he will but grant it to me, he shall never hear the last of it, for as long as I live I will sing his praise; and when the world doth fade away, and the sun grow dim with age, my gratitude, immortal as my soul, shall never cease to sing his love, who pardoned my grossest sins and washed me in his blood." It shall be so. Come and try. Now, sinners, dry your tears; let hopeless sorrows cease; look to the wounds of Christ, who died; let all your griefs now be removed, there is no further cause for them: your Father loves you; he accepts and receives you to his heart.

III. Now, in conclusion, I may notice HOW THESE FEARS WERE MET IN THE PRODIGAL'S CASE, and how they shall be met in ours if we are in the same condition.

The text says, "The Father saw him" Yes, and God saw thee just now. That tear which was wiped away so hastily—as if thou wast ashamed of it—God saw it, and he stored it in his bottle. That prayer which thou didst breathe just a few moments ago, so faintly, and with such little faith—God heard it. The other day thou wast in thy chamber, where no ear heard thee; but God was there. Sinner, let this be thy comfort, that God sees thee when thou beginnest to repent. He does not see thee with his usual gaze, with which he looks on all men; but he sees thee with an eye of intense interest. He has been looking on thee in all thy sin, and in all thy sorrow, hoping that thou wouldst repent; and now he sees the first gleam of grace, and he beholds it with joy. Never warder on the lonely castle top saw the first grey light of morning with more joy than that with which God beholds the first desire in thy heart. Never physician rejoiced more when he saw the first heaving of the lungs in one that was supposed to be dead, than God doth rejoice over thee, now that he sees the first token for good. Think not that thou art despised, and unknown, and forgotten. He is marking thee from his high throne in glory, and rejoicing in what he sees. He saw thee pray, he heard thee groan, he marked thy tear; he looked upon thee and rejoiced to see that these were the first seeds of grace in thine heart.

And then, the text says, "he had compassion on him." He did not merely see him, but he wept within himself to think he should be in such a condition. The old father had a very long range of eye-sight; and though the prodigal could not see him in the distance, he could see the prodigal. And the father's first thought when he saw him was this—"O my poor son, O my poor boy! that ever he should have brought himself into such a state as this!" He looked through his telescope of love, and he saw him, and said, "Ah! he did not go out of my house in such trim as that. Poor creature, his feet are bleeding; he has come a long way, I'll be bound. Look at his face; he doesn't look like the same boy that he was when he left me. His eye that was so bright, is now sunken in its socket; his cheeks that once stood out with fatness, have now become hollow with famine. Poor wretch, I can tell all his bones, he is so emaciated." Instead of feeling any anger in his heart, he felt just the contrary; he felt such pity for his poor son. And that is how the Lord feels for you—you that are groaning and moaning on account of sin. He forgets your sins; he only weeps to think you should have brought yourself to be what you are: "Why didst thou rebel against me, and bring thyself into such a state as this?" It was just like that day when Adam sinned. God walked in the garden, and he missed Adam. He did not cry out, "Adam, come here and be judged!" No; with a soft, sorrowful, and plaintive voice, he said, "Adam, where art thou? Oh, my fair Adam, thou whom I made so happy, where art thou now? Oh, Adam! thou didst think to become a God; where art thou now? Thou hast walked with me; dost thou hide thyself from thy friend? Little dost thou know Oh Adam, what woes thou hast brought on thyself, and thine offspring. Adam, where art thou?" And Jehovah's bowels yearn to-day over you. He is not angry with you; his anger is passed away, and his hands are stretched out still. Inasmuch as he has brought you to feel that you have sinned against him, and to desire reconciliation with him, there is now no wrath in his heart. The only sorrow that he feels is sorrow that you should have brought yourself into a state so mournful as that in which you now are found.

But he did not stop in mere compassion. Having had compassion, "he ran, and fell on his neck, and kissed him." This you do not understand yet; but you shall. As sure as God is God, if you this day are seeking him aright through Christ, the day shall come when the kiss of full assurance shall be on your lip, when the arms of sovereign love shall embrace you, and you shall know it to be so. Thou mayest have despised him, but thou shalt know him yet to be thy Father and thy Friend. Thou mayest have scoffed his name; thou shalt one day come to rejoice in it as better than pure gold. Thou mayest have broken his Sabbaths and despised his Word; the day is coming when the Sabbath shall be thy delight, and his Word thy treasure. Yes, marvel not; thou mayest have plunged into the kennel of sin and made thy clothes black with iniquity; but thou shalt one day stand before his throne white as the angels be; and that tongue that once cursed him shall yet sing his praise. If thou be a real seeker, the hands that have been stained with lust shall one day grasp the harp of gold, and the head that has plotted against the Most High shall yet be girt with gold. Seemeth it not a strange thing that God should do so much for sinners? But strange though it seem, it shall be strangely true. Look at the staggering drunkard in the ale-house. Is there a possibility that one day he shall stand amongst the fairest sons of light? Possibility! ay, certainty, if he repents and turns from the error of his ways. Hear you yon curser and swearer? See you the man who labels himself as a servant of hell, and is not ashamed to do so? Is it possible that he shall one day share the bliss of the redeemed? Possible! ay, more, it is sure, if he turneth from his evil ways. O sovereign grace, turn men that they may repent! "Turn ye, turn ye, why will ye die, O house of Israel?"

"Lord do thou the sinner turn,
For thy tender mercies sake!"

One word or so, and I have done. If any of you to-day are under conviction of sin, let me solemnly warn you not to frequent places where those convictions are likely to be destroyed.

A correspondent of the *New York Christian Advocate* furnishes the following affecting narrative:—

"When I was travelling in the state of Massachusetts, twenty-six years ago, after preaching one evening in the town of ———, a very serious-looking young man arose, and wished to address the assembly. After obtaining leave, he spoke as follows:—'My friends, about one year ago, I set out in company with a young man of my intimate acquaintance, to seek the salvation of my soul. For several weeks we went on together, we laboured together, and often renewed our covenant never to give over seeking till we obtained the religion of Jesus. But, all at once, the young man neglected attending meeting, appeared to turn his back on all the means of grace, and grew so shy of me, that I could scarcely get an opportunity to speak with him. His strange conduct gave me much painful anxiety of mind; but still I felt resolved to obtain the salvation of my soul, or perish, making the publican's plea. After a few days, a friend informed me that my young companion had received an invitation to attend a ball, and was determined to go. I went immediately to him, and, with tears in my eyes, endeavoured to persuade him to change his purpose, and to go with me on that evening to a prayer-meeting. I pleaded with him in vain. He told me, when we parted, that I must not give him up as lost, for after he had attended that ball, he intended to make a business of seeking religion. The appointed evening came, and he went to the ball, and I went to the prayer-meeting. Soon after the meeting opened, it pleased God, in answer to my prayer, to turn my spiritual captivity, and make my soul rejoice in his justifying love. Soon after the ball opened, my young friend was standing at the head of the ball-room, with the hand of a young lady in his hand, preparing to lead down the dance; and, while the musician was turning his violin, without one moment's warning, the young man sallied back, and fell dead on the floor. I was immediately sent for, to assist in devising means to convey his remains to his father's house. You will be better able to judge what were the emotions of my heart, when I tell you that that young man was my own brother.'"

Trifle not, then, with thy convictions, for eternity shall be too short for thee to utter thy lamentations over such trifling.

Metropolitan Tabernacle Pulpit.

THE PRODIGAL'S RECEPTION.

A Sermon

DELIVERED ON SUNDAY MORNING, SEPTEMBER 4TH, 1864, BY

C. H. SPURGEON,

AT THE METROPOLITAN TABERNACLE, NEWINGTON.

"And he arose, and came to his father. But when he was yet a great way off his father saw him, and had compassion, and ran, and fell on his neck, and kissed him."—Luke xv. 20.

THERE he is! he is as wretched as misery itself; as filthy as his brute associates who could satisfy themselves with husks, while he could not. His clothes hang about him in rags, and what he is without, that he is within. He is disgraced in the eyes of the good, and the virtuous remember him with indignation. He has some desires to go back to his father's house; but *these desires are not sufficient to alter his condition.* Mere desires have not scraped the filth from him, nor have they so much as patched his rags. Whatever he may or may not desire, he is still filthy, still disgraced, still an alien from his father's house: and he knows it, for he has come to himself. He would have been angry if we had said as much as this before, but now we cannot describe him in words too black. With many tears and sighs he assures us that he is even worse than he appears to be, and that no man can know all the depth of the vileness of his conduct: he has spent his living with harlots; he has despised a generous parent's love and broken lose from his wise control; he has done evil with both his hands to the utmost of his strength and opportunity. There he stands, notwithstanding this confession, just what I have described him to be; for even though he has said within himself, "I have sinned," yet *that confession has not removed his griefs.* He acknowledges that he is not worthy to be called a son—and it is true he is not; but his unworthiness is not removed by his consciousness of it, nor by his confession of it. He has no claims to a father's love. If that father shuts the door in his face, he acts with justice to him; if he shall refuse so much as to speak a single word, except words of rebuke, no one can blame the father, for the son has so sadly erred. To this the son utters no demur; he confesses that if he be cast away for ever, he deserves it well. This picture, I know, is the photograph of some who are now present. You feel your vileness and sinfulness, but you cannot look upon that sense of vileness as in any way extenuating or altering your condition. You feel, but you cannot plead your feelings. You confess this morning that you have desires towards God, but that you have no rights to him—you cannot demand anything at his hands. If your soul were sent to hell, his righteous law approves it, and so does your own conscience. You can see your rags, you can mark your filthiness, you can long for something better, but you *are* no better; you have no more claims than you used to have upon God's mercy; you stand here to-day, a self-convicted offender against the lovingkindness and holiness of God. I pray that to such of you as are in this case, I may be the bearer of a message from God to your soul this morning. O you who know the Lord, put up earnest and silent prayers just now, that my message may come home with power to troubled consciences; and I beseech you, for your own profit, look back to the hole of the pit whence ye were digged, and to the miry clay whence ye were drawn, and remember how God received you. And while we talk of what he is willing and able to do to the far off sinners, let your souls leap with joyous gratitude at the recollection of how he received you into his love, and made you partakers of his grace in days gone by.

There are two things in the text: the first is *the condition of many a seeker—he is yet a great way off;* and then, secondly, *the matchless kindness of the father towards him.*

I. First, dear friends, THE CONDITION OF SUCH A SEEKER—HE IS YET A GREAT WAY OFF.

He is a great way off if you consider one or two things. Remember *his want of strength.* This poor young man had for some time been without food—brought so very low that the husks upon which the swine fed would have seemed a dainty to him if he could have eaten them. He is so hungry that he has become emaciated, and to him every mile has the weariness of leagues within it. It costs him many pains and sore griefs to drag himself along, even though it be but an inch. So the sinner is a long way off from God when you consider his utter want of strength to come to God. Even such strength as God has given him is very painfully used. God has given him strength enough to desire salvation, but those desires are always accompanied with deep and sincere grief for sin. The point which he has already reached has exhausted all his power, and all he can do is to fall down before Jesus, and say,

"Oh! for this no strength have I,
My strength is at thy feet to lie."

He is a great way off again, if you consider *his want of courage.* He longs to see his father, but yet the probabilities are that if his father should come he would run away: the very sound of his father's footsteps would act upon him as they did on Adam in the garden—he would hide himself among the trees; so that instead of crying after his father, the great Father would have to cry after him—"Where art thou, poor fallen creature? where art thou?" His want of courage, therefore, makes the distance long, for every step hitherto has been taken as though into the jaws of death. "Ah!" saith the sinner, "it must be long before I can dare to hope, for mine inquities have gone over my head so that I cannot look up." Are you then in alarm and dread this morning? Your prayers seem to yourself to have been no prayers at all; when you think of God, terror comes over your mind, and you feel that you are a long, long way from him; you imagine that it is not likely that he will hear your cries nor give heed to your words. You are yet a great way off.

You are a great way off when we consider *the difficulty of the way of repentance.* John Bunyan tells us that Christian found, when he went back to the arbour after his lost roll, that it was very hard work going back. Every backslider finds it so, and every penitent sinner knows that there is a bitterness in mourning for sin comparable to the loss of one's only son. A drowning man feels no great pain: the sensations of drowning are even said to be pleasant; it is only when the man is being restored to life, when the blood begins to make the veins tingle because life leaps there, when once again the nerves are sensible, then we are told that the whole body is full of many agonies, but then they are the agonies of life: and so the poor penitent feels the goal must be a great way, for if he had to feel as he now feels, even for a month, it were a great time; and if he had to journey many miles as he now journeys, so painfully, with such bleeding feet, it would indeed be a great way.

Let us look into this matter, and show that while the road seems long on this account, *it really is long* if we view it in certain lights. There are many seeking sinners who are a great way off in *their life.* I think I see the man now, and hear him thus bewail himself, "I have left off my drunkenness. I could not sit where I used to sit by the hour. I thank God I shall never be seen reeling through the streets again, for that grovelling lust I detest. I have given up Sabbath-breaking, and I am found in God's house; and I have endeavoured, as much as I can, to renounce the habit of swearing, but still I am a great way off; I do not feel as if I could yet lay hold of Christ, for I cannot master my own passions yet. An old companion stopped me this week, and he had not long been talking before I found the old man was in me, and the old lustings came up into my face again. Why, sir, the other day an oath came rapping out. I thought I had got over it, but I had not—I am a great way off. When I read of what saints are, and observe what true Christians are, I do feel that my conduct is so inconsistent and so widely apart from what it ought to be, that I am a great way off." Ah! dear friend, you are; and if you had to come to God by the way of your own righteousness you would never reach him, for he is not thus to be found. Christ Jesus is the way. He is the safe, sure, and perfect road to God. He who sees Jesus, has seen the Father; but he who looks to himself will only see despair. The road to heaven by Mount Sinai is impassable by mortal man, but Calvary leads to glory; the secret places of the stairs are in the wounds of Jesus.

Again, you feel yourself a great way off as to *knowledge.* "Why," say you, "before I felt thus I considered myself a master of all theology: I could twist the doctrines round my fingers. When I listened to a sermon I felt quite able to criticize it, and to give my judgment. Now I see that my judgment was about as valuable as the criticism of a blind man upon a picture, for I was without spiritual sight.

Now I feel myself to be a fool. I do know what sin means, but only to a degree. Even here I feel that I am not conscious of the heinousness of human guilt. I have heard the doctrine of the atonement of Christ, and I thank God I know it to some degree, but the excellence and glory of the substitutionary sacrifice which Christ offered I confess I do not fully comprehend." The sinner's confession now is that instead of understanding Scripture he finds he needs to go like a child to school to learn the A B C of it. "O sir," says he, "I am a great way off from God, for I am so ignorant, so foolish, I seem to be but as a beast when I think of the deep things of God." Ah! poor soul, poor young wandering brother, I wonder not that it seems so to you, for the ignorance of the carnal man is indeed fearful, and only God can give thee light; but he can give it to thee in a moment, and the distance between thee and him upon the score of ignorance can be bridged at once, and thou mayst comprehend even to-day, with all saints, what are the heights and depths, and know the love of Christ which passeth knowledge.

In another point also many an earnest seeker is a great way off, I mean in *his repentance*. "Alas!" says he, "I cannot repent as I ought. If I could feel the brokenness of heart which I have heard and seen in some! Oh! what would I give for penitential sighs; how thankful should I be if my head were waters, and mine eyes fountains of tears, if I could even feel that I was as humble as the poor publican, and could stand with downcast eyes and beat upon my breast and say, 'God be merciful to me a sinner.' But, alas! I have been a hearer of the Word for years, and all the progress I have made is so little, that while I know the gospel to be true, I do not feel it. I know myself to be a sinner, and sometimes I mourn over it, but my mourning is so superficial, my repentance is a repentance that needs to be repented of. O sir, if God would use the heaviest hammer that he had, if he would but break my heart, every broken fragment should bless his name. I wish I had a genuine repentance. Oh! how I pant to be brought to feel that I am lost, and to desire Christ with that vehement desire which will not take a denial; but in this point my heart seems hard as hell-hardened steel, cold as a rock of ice, it will not, cannot yield, though wooed by love divine. Adamant itself may run in liquid torrents, but my soul yields to nothing. Lord, break it! Lord, break it!!" Ah! poor heart, I see thou art a great way off, but dost thou know if my Lord should appear to thee this morning, and say to thee, "I have loved thee with an everlasting love," thine heart would break in a moment?

> "Law and terrors do but harden,
> All the while they work alone;
> But a sense of blood-bought pardon,
> Can dissolve a heart of stone."

Great way off as you are, if the Lord pardons you, while yet callous, and consciously hard of heart, will you not then fall at his feet and commend that great love wherewith he loved you, even when ye were dead in trespasses and sins?

Yes, but I think I hear one say, "There is another point in which I feel a great way off, for I have little or no *faith.* I have heard faith preached every Sabbath day; I know what it is, I think I do, but I cannot reach it. I know that if I cast myself wholly upon Christ I shall be saved. I quite comprehend that he does not ask anything of me, any willings, or doings, or feelings: I know that Christ is willing to receive the greatest sinner out of hell if that sinner will but come and simply trust him. I have tried to do it; sometimes I have thought I had faith, but then again when I have looked at my sins I have doubted so dreadfully, that I perceive I have no faith at all. There are sunshiny moments with me when I think I can say—

> "My faith is built on nothing less,
> Than Jesus' blood and righteousness."

but oh! when I feel my corruptions within rising upon me, I hear a voice saying, "The Philistines be upon thee, Samson," and straightway I discover my own weakness. I have not the faith that I want; I am a great way off from it, and I fear that I shall never possess it. Yes, my brethren, I perceive your difficulty, for I have felt the sorrow of it myself; but oh! my Lord, who is the giver of faith, who is exalted on high to give repentance and remission of sins, can give you the faith you so much desire, and can cause you this morning to rest with perfect confidence upon the work which he has finished for you.

To gather up all things in one word, the truly penitent sinner feels that he is yet a great way off *in everything.* There is no point upon which you can talk with him but it will be sure to lead to a confession of his deficiency. Begin to put him in the scales of the sanctuary, and he cries, "Alas! before you put in the weights I can tell you I shall be found wanting." Bring him to the touchstone, and he shrinks from it; "Nay," says he, "but I cannot endure any sort of trial—

> 'All unholy and unclean,
> I am nothing else but sin.'"

See, see, how well my Master has pictured your case in this parable—"Yet a great way off," yet covered with rags, yet polluted with filth, yet in disgrace, yet a stranger to your Father's house, there is only this one point about you, you have your face towards your Father, you have a desire towards God, and you would, oh! you would if you could, lay hold upon eternal life. But you feel too far off for anything like comfortable hope; now I must confess I feel many fears about you who are in this state; I am afraid lest you should come so far and yet go back; for there are many whom we thought had come as far as this, and yet they have gone back after all. Oh! remember that desires after God will not change you so as to save you. You must find Christ. Remember that to say, "I will arise" is not enough, nor even to arise; you must never rest till your Father has given you the kiss, till he has put on you the best robe. I am afraid lest you should rest satisfied and say, "I am in a good state; the minister tells us that many are brought to such a state before they are saved. I will stop here." My dear friend, it is a good state *to pass through,* but it is a bad state *to rest in.* I pray you never be content with a sense of sin, never be satisfied with merely knowing that you are not what you ought to be. It never cures the fever for a man to know he has it; his knowledge is in some degree a good sign, for it proves that the fever has not yet driven him to delirium; but it never gives a man perfect health to know that he is sick. It is a good thing for him to know it, for he will not otherwise send for the physician; but except it lead to that, he will die whether he feels himself to be sick or no. A mere consciousness that you are hungry while your father's hired servants have bread enough and to spare, will not stay your hunger, you want more than this. You are a great way off, and I beseech you remember the danger is, lest you should stop here or should lose what sensibility you already have. Perhaps despair may come upon you. Some have commited suicide while under a sense of the greatness of their distance from God, because they dared not look to the Saviour. Our prayers shall go up to God that the second part of our text may come true to you, and that alike backsliding and despair may be prevented by the speedy coming of God dressed in the robes of grace to meet your guilty soul, and give you joy and peace through believing.

II. Secondly—and O may the Master give us his help—we have to consider THE MATCHLESS KINDNESS OF THE HEAVENLY FATHER. We must take each word and dwell upon it.

First of all, we have here *divine observation.* "When he was yet a great way off *his father saw him.*" It is true he has always seen him. God sees the sinner in every state and in every position. Ay, and sees him with an eye of love too—such a chosen sinner as is described in this text—not with complacency, but still with affection. God looks upon his wandering chosen ones. I say that father saw his son when he spent his living with harlots, saw him with deep sorrow, when he fain would have filled his belly with the husks which the swine did eat; but now, if there can be such a thing as for divine omniscience to become more exact, the father sees him with an eye full of a more tender love, a greater care. "His father saw *him.*" Oh! what a sight it was for a father to see! His son, it is true, but his reprobate son, who had dishonoured his father's name; brought down the name of an honourable house to be mentioned among the dregs and scum of the earth. There he is! What a sight for a *father's* eye! He is filthy, as though he had been rolling in the mire; and his gay clothing has long ago lost its fine colours, and hangs about him in wretched rags. The father does not turn away and try to forget him, he fixes his full gaze upon him. Sinner, thou knowest that God sees thee this morning; sitting in this house thou art observed of the God of heaven. There is not a desire in thy heart unread of him, nor a tear in thine eye which he doth not observe. I tell thee he has seen thy midnight sins, he has heard thy cursings and thy blasphemies, and yet he has loved thee notwithstanding all that thou hast done. Thou couldst hardly have been a worse rebel against him, and yet he has noted thee in his book of love, and determined to save thee, and the eye of his love has followed thee whithersoever thou hast gone. Is there not some comfort here? Why could not *he* see his father? Was it the effect of the tears in his eyes that he could not see? or was it that his father was of quicker sight than he? Sinner, thou canst not see God, for thou art unbelieving, and carnal, and blind, but he can see thee; thy tears of penitence block up thy sight, but thy Father is quick of eye, and he beholds thee and loves thee now; in every glance there is love. "His father saw him."

Observe this was a loving observation, for it is written, "*His father* saw him." He did not see him as a mere casual observer; he did not note him as a man might note his friend's child with some pity and benevolence, but he marked him as a father alone can do. What a quick eye a parent hath! Why, I have known a young man come home, perhaps for a short holiday: the mother has heard nothing, not even a whisper, as to her son's conduct, and yet she cannot help observing to her husband, "There is a something about John which makes me suspect that he is not going on as he should do. I do not know, my husband," she says, "what it is, but yet I am sure he is getting among bad companions." She will read his character at once. And the father notes something, too, he cannot precisely say what, but cause for anxiety he knows it to be. But here we have a Father who can see everything, and who has as much of the quickness of love as he has of the certainty of knowledge. He can, therefore, see from every spot and bruise, and note every putrifying sore. He sees his poor son right through as though he were a vase of crystal; he reads his heart, not merely the tell-tale garments, not merely the sorrowful tale of the unwashed face and those clouted shoes, but he can read his soul, he understands the whole of his miserable plight. O poor sinner, there is no need for thee to give information to thy God, for he knows it already; you need not pick your words in prayer in order to make your case plain and perspicuous, for God can see it, and all you have to do is to uncover your wounds, your bruises, and your putrifying sores, and say, "My Father, thou seest it all, the black tale thou readest in a moment, my Father, have pity upon me."

The next thought to be well considered is *divine compassion.* "When he saw him he had compassion on him." Does not the word *com-passion* mean *suffering-with* or *fellow-suffering?* What is compassion, then, but putting yourself into the place of the sufferer and feeling his grief?

If I may so say, the father put himself into the son's rags, and then felt as much pity for him as that poor ragged prodigal could have felt for himself. I do not know how to bring up your compassion this morning, except it is by supposing that it is your own case. I will suppose, father, it is a son of yours. I saw, not many hours ago, a young man who brought to my mind the prodigal in this case: his face marked with innumerable lines of sin and wretchedness, his body lean and emaciated, his clothes close-buttoned, his whole appearance the very mirror of woe. He knocked at my door. I knew his case; I cannot hurt him by telling it. He had disgraced his family, not once nor twice, but many times. At last he drew out what money he had in the business of a respectable family, came up to London with four hundred pounds, and in about five weeks spent it all; and, without a single farthing to help himself, he often wants for bread, and I fear that he has often crept at night into the parks to sleep, and thus has brought aches and pains into his bones which will hold by him till he dies. He wanders the streets by day a vagabond and a reprobate. I have written to his friends, the case has been put before them; they will not own him; and considering his shameful conduct, I do not wonder at it. He has no father and no mother left. If he were helped beyond mere food and lodging, as far as we can judge, it would be money thrown away; if he were helped, he seems so desperately set on wickedness, that he would do the same again. Yet, as I think, I can but desire to see him have one more trial at the least, and he would have it, I doubt not, if *his father* yet lived; but others feel the fountains of their love are stayed. As I think of him, I cannot but feel that if he were a son of mine and I were his father, and I saw him in such a case come to my door, whatever the crime was that he had committed, I must fall upon his neck and kiss him; the hugest sin could not put out for ever the sparks of paternal love. I might condemn the sin in terms the sharpest and most severe; I might regret that he had ever been born, and cry with David, "O my son Absalom, my son, my son Absalom! would God I had died for thee!" but I could not shut him out of my house, nor refuse to call him my child. My child he is, and my child he shall be till he dies. You feel just now that if it were your child you would do the same. That is how God feels towards you, his chosen, his repentant child. You *are* his child; I hope so, I trust so; those desires which you have in your soul towards him, make me feel that you are one of his children, and as God looks out of heaven he knows what you mean. What is it? What shall I say? Nay, I need not describe, but, "Like as a father pitieth his children, so the Lord pitieth them that fear him." He will have compassion upon you; he will receive you to his bosom now. Be of good courage, for the text says, "He had compassion on him."

Notice and observe carefully *the swiftness of this divine love:*—"He ran." Probably he was walking on the top of his house and looking out for his son, when one morning he just caught a glimpse of a poor sorry figure in the distance. If he had been anything but the father he would not have known it to be his son, he was so altered; but he looked and looked again, till at last he said, "It is he! oh! what marks of famine are upon him, and of suffering too!" And down comes the old gentleman—I think I see him running downstairs, and the servants come to the windows and the doors, and say, "Where is master going? I have not seen him run at that rate for many a-day." See, there he goes; he does not take the road, for that is a little round about; but there is a gap through the hedge, and he is jumping over it; the straightest way that he can find he chooses; and before the son has had time to notice who it is, he is on him, and has his arms about him, falling upon his neck and kissing him. I recollect a young prodigal who was received in the same way. Here he stands, it is I, myself. I sat in a little chapel, little dreaming that *my Father* saw me; certainly I was a great way off. I felt something of my need of Christ, but I did not know what I must do to be saved; though taught the letter of the Word, I was spiritually ignorant of the plan of salvation; though taught it from my youth up, I knew it not. I felt, but I did not feel what I wished to feel. If ever there was a soul that knew itself to be far off from God, I was that soul; and yet in a moment, in one single moment, no sooner had I heard the words, "Look unto me and be ye saved, all the ends of the earth," no sooner had I turned my eyes to Jesus crucified, than I felt my perfect reconciliation with God, I knew my sins to be forgiven. There was no time for getting out of my heavenly Father's way, it was done, and done in an instant; and in my case, at least, he ran and fell upon my neck to kiss me. I hope that will be the case this morning; before you can get out of this place, before you can get back to your old doubtings, and fearings, and sighings, and cryings, I hope here the Lord of love will run and meet you, and fall upon your neck and kiss you.

After noticing thus, *observation*, *compassion*, and *swiftness*, do not forget *the nearness:* "He fell upon his neck and kissed him." This I can understand by experience, but it is too wonderful for me to explain, "he fell upon his neck." If he had stood at a distance and said, "John, I should be very glad to kiss you, but you are too filthy; I do not know what may be under those filthy rags; I do not feel inclined to fall upon your neck just yet; you are too far gone for me. I love you, but there is a limit to the display of love. When I have got you into a proper state, then I may manifest my affection to you, but I cannot just now, while you are so very foul." Oh! no; but before he is washed he falls on his neck—there is the wonder of it. I can understand how God manifests his love to a soul that is washed in Jesus' blood, and knows it; but how he could fall upon the neck of a foul, filthy sinner *as such!* There it is—not as sanctified, not as having anything good in himself, but as nothing but a filthy, foul, desperate rebel, God falls upon his neck and kisses him. Oh! strange miracle of love! The riddle is unriddled when you recollect that God never had looked upon that sinner, as he was in himself, but had always looked upon him as he was in Christ; and when he fell upon that prodigal's neck, he did in effect only fall upon the neck of his once-suffering Son, Jesus Christ, and he kissed the sinner because he saw him in Christ, and therefore did not see the sinner's loathsomeness, but saw only Christ's comeliness, and therefore kissed him as he would have kissed his substitute. Observe how near God comes to the sinner. It was said of that eminent saint and martyr, Bishop Hooper, that on one occasion a man in deep distress was allowed to go into his prison to tell his tale of conscience; but Bishop Hooper looked so sternly upon him, and addressed him so severely at first, that the poor soul ran away, and could not get comfort until he had sought out another minister of a gentler aspect. Now Hooper really was a gracious and loving soul, but the sternness of his manner kept the penitent off. There is no such stern manner in our heavenly Father, he loves to receive his prodigals. When he comes there is no "Hold off!" no "Keep off!" to the sinner, but he falls upon his neck and he kisses him.

There is yet another thought to be brought out of the metaphor of kissing; we are not to pass that over without dipping our cup in the honey. In kissing his son the father *recognises relationship.* He said, with emphasis, "Thou art my son," and the prodigal was

"To his Father's bosom pressed,
Once for all a child confessed."

Again, that kiss was the seal of *forgiveness.* He would not have kissed him if he had been angry with him; he forgave him, forgave him all. There was, moreover, something more than forgiveness, there was *acceptance*—"I receive you back into my heart as though you were worthy of all that I give to your elder brother, and therefore I kiss you." Surely also this was a kiss of delight—as if he took pleasure in him, delighting in him, feasting his eyes with the sight of him, and feeling more happy to see him than to see all his fields, and the fatted calves, and all the treasures that he possessed. His delight was in seeing this poor restored child. Surely this is all summed up in a kiss. And if this morning my Father, and your Father, should come out to meet mourning penitents, in a moment he will show you that you are his children, you shall say, "Abba, Father," on your road to your own house; you shall feel that your sin is all forgiven, that every particle of it is cast behind

Jehovah's back; you shall feel to-day that you are accepted—as your faith looks to Christ you shall see that God accepts you, because Christ your substitute is worthy of God's love and God's delight. Nay; I trust you shall this very morning delight yourself in God, because God delights himself in you, and you shall hear him whisper in your ear, "Thou shalt be called Hephzi-bah . . . for the Lord delighteth in thee." I wish I could picture such a text as this as it ought to be; it needs some tender, sympathetic heart, some man who is the very soul of pathos, to work out the tender touches of such a verse as this. But, oh! though I cannot describe it, I hope you will feel it, and that is better than description. I come not here to paint the scene, except to be the brush in God's hand to paint it on your hearts. There are some of you who can say, "I do not want descriptions, for I have felt it; I went to Christ and told him my case, and prayed him to meet me; now I believe on him, and I have gone my way rejoicing in him."

We will just say these words and have done. In summing up, one may notice that this sinner, though he was a great way off, was *not received to full pardon and to adoption and acceptance by a gradual process, but he was received at once.* He was not allowed to enter into the out-house first, and to sleep in a barn at night, and then afterwards allowed to come sometimes and have his meals with the servants in the kitchen, and then afterwards allowed to sit at the bottom of the table and by degrees brought near. No; but the father fell on his neck and kissed him the first moment; he gets as near to God the first moment as he ever will. So a saved soul may not enjoy and know so much, but he is as near and dear to God the first moment he believes as he ever will be; a true heir of all things in Christ, and as truly so as even when he shall mount to heaven to be glorified and to be like his Lord. Oh! what a wonder is this? Fresh from his pigstye was he not, yet in a father's bosom; fresh from the swine with their gruntings in his ears, and now he hears a father's loving words; a few days ago he was putting husks to his mouth, and now it is a father's lips that are on his lips. What a change, and all at once. I say there is no gradual process in this, but the thing is done at once, in a moment he comes to his father, his father comes to him, and he is in his father's arms.

Observe again, as there was not a gradual reception, there was *not a partial reception.* He was not forgiven on conditions; he was not received to his father's heart if he would do so-and-so. No; there were no "ifs" and no "buts;" he was kissed, and clothed, and feasted, without a single condition of any kind whatever. No questions asked—his father had cast his offences behind his back in a moment, and he was received without even a censure or a rebuke. It was not a partial reception. He was not received to some things and refused others. He was not, for instance, allowed to call himself a child, but to think himself an inferior. No; he wears the best robe; he has the ring on his finger; he has the shoes on his feet; and he joins in eating the fatted calf; and so the sinner is not received to a second class place, but he is taken to the full position of a child of God. It is not a gradual nor yet a partial reception.

And once more, it is *not a temporary reception.* His father did not kiss him and then turn him out at the back door. He did not receive him for a time, and then afterwards say to him, "Go thy way; I have had pity upon thee; thou hast now a new start, go into the far country and mend thy ways." No; but the father would say to him what he had already said to the elder brother, "Son, thou art ever with me, and all that I have is thine." In the parable, the son could not have the goods restored, for he had spent his part; but in the truth itself and matter of fact, God does make the man who comes in at the eleventh hour equal with the one who came in at the first hour of the day; he gives every man the penny; and he gives to the child who has been the most wandering the same privileges, and ultimately the same heritage, which he gives to his own who have been these many years with him, and have not transgressed his commandments. That is a remarkable passage in one of the prophets, where he says, "Ekron as a Jebusite;" meaning that the Philistine when converted should be treated just the same as the original inhabitants of Jerusalem; that the branches of the olive which were grafted in have the same privileges as the original branches. When God takes men from being heirs of wrath, and makes them heirs of grace, they have just as much privilege at the first as though they had been heirs of grace twenty years, because in God's sight they always were heirs of grace, and from all eternity he viewed his most wandering sons.

"Not as they stood in Adam's fall,
When sin and ruin covered all;
But as they'll stand another day,
Fairer than sun's meridian ray."

O, I would to God that he would in his infinite mercy bring some of his own dear children home this day, and he shall have the praise, world without end. Amen.

Metropolitan Tabernacle Pulpit.

THE TURNING POINT.

A Sermon

DELIVERED ON LORD'S-DAY MORNING, AUGUST 23RD, 1874, BY

C. H. SPURGEON,

AT THE METROPOLITAN TABERNACLE, NEWINGTON.

"And he arose, and came to his father."—Luke xv. 20.

THIS sentence expresses the true turning point in the prodigal's life story. Many other matters led up to it, and before he came to it there was much in him that was very hopeful; but this was the point itself, and had he never reached it he would have remained a prodigal, but would never have been the prodigal restored, and his life would have been a warning rather than an instruction to us. "He arose, and came to his father." Speaking, as I do, in extreme weakness, I have no words to spare; and while my voice holds out I shall speak straight to the point, and I pray the Lord to make every syllable practical and powerful by his Holy Spirit.

I. We shall begin by noticing that HERE WAS ACTION—"*He arose, and came to his father.*" He had already been in a state of thoughtfulness; he had come to himself, but now he was to go further, and come to his father. He had considered the past, and weighed it up, and seen the hollowness of all the world's pleasures; he had seen his condition in reference to his father, and his prospects if he remained in the far-off country; he had thought upon what he ought to do, and what would be the probable result of such a course; but now he passed beyond the dreaminess of thought into matter-of-fact acting and doing. How long will it be, dear hearers, before you will do the same? We are glad to have you thoughtful; we hope that a great point is gained when you are led to consider your ways, to ponder your condition, and to look earnestly into the future, for thoughtlessness is the ruin of many a traveller to eternity, and by its means the unwary fall into the deep pit of carnal security and perish therein. But some of you have been among the "thoughtful" quite long enough; it is time you passed into a more practical stage. It is high time that you came to action; it would have been better if you had acted already; for, in the matter of reconciliation to God, first thoughts are best. When a man's life hangs on a thread, and hell is just before him, his path is clear, and a second thought is superfluous. The first impulse to escape from danger and lay hold on Christ is that which you would be wise to follow. Some of you whom I now address have been thinking, and thinking, and thinking, till I fear that you will think yourselves into perdition. May you, by divine grace, be turned from thinking to believing, or else your thoughts will become the undying worm of your torment.

The prodigal had also passed beyond mere regret. He was deeply grieved that he had left his father's house, he lamented his lavish expenditure upon wantonness and revelling, he mourned that the son of such a father should be degraded into a swineherd in a foreign land; but he now proceeded from regret to repentance, and bestirred himself to escape from the condition over which he mourned. What is the use of regret if we continue in sin? By all means pull up the sluices of your grief if the floods will turn the wheel of action, but you may as well reserve your tears, if they mean no more than idle sentimentalism. What avails it for a man to say he repents of his misconduct if he still perseveres in it? We are glad when sinners regret their sin and mourn the condition into which sin has brought them, but if they go no further, their regrets will only prepare them for eternal remorse. Had the prodigal become inactive through despondency, or stolid through sullen grief, he must have perished, far away from his father's home, as it is to be feared many will whose sorrow for sin leads them into a proud unbelief and wilful despair of God's love; but he was wise, for he shook off the drowsiness of his despondency, and, with resolute determination, "arose and came to his father." Oh, when will you sad ones be wise enough to do the same? When will your thinking and your sorrowing give place to practical obedience to the gospel?

The prodigal also pressed beyond mere resolving. That is a sweet verse which says, "I will arise," but that is far better which says, "And he arose." Resolves are good, like blossoms, but actions are better, for they are the fruits. We are glad to hear from you the resolution, "I will turn to God," but holy angels in heaven do not rejoice over resolutions, they reserve their music for sinners who actually repent. Many of you like the son in the parable have said, "I go, sir," but you have not gone. You are as ready at forgetting as you are at resolving. Every earnest sermon, every death in your family, every funeral knell for a neighbour, every pricking of conscience, every touch of sickness, sets you a resolving to amend, but your promissory notes are never honoured, your repentance ends in words. Your goodness is as the dew, which at early dawn hangs each blade of grass with gems, but leaves the fields all parched and dry when the sun's burning heat is poured upon the pasture. You mock your friends, and trifle with your own souls. You have often in this house said, "Let me reach my chamber and I will fall upon my knees," but on the way home you have forgotten what manner of men you were, and sin has confirmed its tottering throne. Have you not dallied long enough? Have you not lied unto God sufficiently? Should you not now give over resolving and proceed to the solemn business of your souls like men of common sense? You are in a sinking vessel, and the life-boat is near, but your mere resolve to enter it will not prevent your going down with the sinking craft; as sure as you are a living man, you will drown unless you take the actual leap for life.

"He arose and came to his father." Now, observe that *this action of the prodigal was immediate*, and without further parley. He did not go back to the citizen of that country and say, "Will you raise my wages? If not, I must leave." Had he parleyed he had been lost; but he gave his old master no notice, he cancelled his indentures by running away. I would that sinners here would break their league with death, and violate their covenant with hell, by escaping for their lives to Jesus, who receives all such runaways. We want neither leave nor licence for quitting the service of sin and Satan, neither is it a subject which demands a month's consideration: in this matter instantaneous action is the surest wisdom. Lot did not stop to consult the king of Sodom as to whether he might quit his dominions, neither did he consult the parish officers as to the propriety of speedily deserting his home; but with the angel's hand pressing them, he and his fled from the city. Nay, one fled not; she looked and lingered, and that lingering cost her her life! That pillar of salt is the eloquent monitor to us to avoid delays when we are bidden to flee for our lives. Sinner, dost thou wish to be a pillar of salt? Wilt thou halt between two opinions, until God's anger shall doom thee to final impenitence? Wilt thou trifle with mercy till justice smite thee? Up, man, and while thy day of grace continues, fly thou into the arms of love.

The text implies that *the prodigal aroused himself*, and put forth all his energies. It is said, "he *arose*;" the word suggests that he had till then been asleep upon the bed of sloth, or the couch of presumption. Like Samson in Delilah's lap, he had been supine, inactive, and unstrung; but now, startled from his lethargy, he lifts up his eyes, he girds up his loins, he shakes off the spell which had enthralled him, he puts forth every power, he arouses his whole nature, and he spares no exertion until he returns to his father.

Men are not saved between sleeping and waking. "The kingdom of heaven suffereth violence, and the violent take it by force." Grace does not stupefy us, it but arouses us. Surely, sirs, it is worth while making an awful effort to escape from eternal wrath. It is worth while summoning up every faculty and power and emotion and passion of your being, and saying to yourself, "I cannot be lost; I will not be lost: I am resolved that I will find mercy through Jesus Christ." The worst of it is, O sinners, ye are so sluggish, so indifferent, so ready to let things happen as they may. Sin has bewitched and benumbed you. You sleep as on beds of down and forget that you are in danger of hell fire. You cry, "A little more rest, and a little more slumber, and a little more folding of the arms to sleep," and so you sleep on, though your damnation slumbereth not. Would to God you could be awakened. It is not in the power of my voice to arouse you; but may the Lord Himself alarm you, for never were men more in danger. Let but your breath fail, or your blood pause, and you are lost for ever. Frailer than a cobweb is that life on which your eternal destiny depends. If you were wise you would not give sleep to your eyes, nor slumber to your eyelids, till you had found your God and been forgiven. Oh, when will you come to a real action? How long will it be ere you believe in Jesus? How long will you sport between the jaws of hell? How long dare you provoke the living God?

II. Secondly, HERE WAS A SOUL COMING INTO ACTUAL CONTACT WITH GOD,—"*He arose and came to his father.*" It would have been of no avail for him to have arisen if he had not come to his father. This is what the sinner has to do, and what the Spirit enables him to do: namely, to come straight away to his God. But, alas! very commonly, when men begin to be anxious, they go round about and hasten to a friend to tell him about it, or they even resort to a deceitful priest, and seek help from him. They fly to a saint or a virgin, and ask these to be mediators for them, instead of accepting the only Mediator Jesus Christ, and going to God at once by him. They fly to outward forms and ceremonies, or they turn to their Bibles, their prayers, their repentances, or their sermon-hearings; in fact, to anything rather than their God. But the prodigal knew better; he went to his father, and it will be a grand day for you, O sinner, when you do the same. Go straight away to your God in Christ Jesus. "Come here," says the priest. Pass that fellow by. Get away to your Father. Reject an angel from heaven if he would detain you from the Lord. Go personally, directly, and at once to God in Christ Jesus. But surely I must perform some ceremony first? Not so did the prodigal, he arose and went at once to his father. Sinner, you must come to God, and Jesus is the way; go to him then, tell him you have done wrong, confess your sins to him, and yield yourself to him. Cry, "Father, I have sinned: forgive me, for Jesus' sake."

Alas! there are many anxious souls who do not go to others, but they look to themselves. They sit down and cry, "I want to repent; I want to feel my need; I want to be humble." O man, get up! What are you at? Leave yourself and go to your Father. "Oh, but I have so little hope; my faith is very weak, and I am full of fears." What matters your hopes or your fears while you are away from your Father? Your salvation does not lie within yourself, but in the Lord's good will to you. You will never be at peace till, leaving all your doubts and your hopes, you come to your God and rest in his bosom. "Oh, but I want to conquer my propensities to sin, I want to master my strong temptations." I know what it is you want. You want the best robe without your Father's giving it you, and shoes on your feet of your own procuring; you do not like going in a beggar's suit and receiving all from the Lord's loving hand; but this pride of yours must be given up, and you must get away to God, or perish for ever. You must forget yourself, or only remember yourself so as to feel that you are bad throughout, and no more worthy to be called God's son. Give yourself up as a sinking vessel that is not worth pumping, but must be left to go down, and get you into the life-boat of free grace. Think of God your Father—of him, I say, and of his dear Son, the one Mediator and Redeemer of the sons of men. There is your hope—to fly away from self and to reach your Father.

Do I hear you say, "Well, I shall continue in the means of grace, and I hope there to find my God." I tell you, if you do that, and refuse to go to God, the means of grace will be the means of damnation to you. "I must wait at the pool," says one. Then I solemnly warn you that you will lie there and die; for Jesus does not command you to lie there, his bidding is, "Take up thy bed, and walk." "Believe in the Lord Jesus Christ, and thou shalt be saved." You have to go unto your Father, and not to the pool of Bethesda, or any other pool of ordinances or means of grace. "But I mean to pray," says one. What would you pray for? Can you expect the Lord to hear you while you will not hear him? You will pray best with your head in your Father's bosom, but the prayers of an unyielding, disobedient, unbelieving heart are mockeries. Prayers themselves will ruin you if they are made a substitute for going at once to God. Suppose the prodigal had sat down at the swine trough and said, "I will pray here," what would it have availed him? or suppose he had wept there, what good would have come of it? Praying and weeping were good enough when he had come to his father, but they could not have been substituted for it. Sinner, your business is with God. Hasten tc him at once. You have nothing to do with yourself, or your own doings, or what others can do for you, the turning point of salvation is, "he arose and came to his father." There must be a real, living, earnest, contact of your poor guilty soul with God, a recognition that there is a God, and that God can be spoken to, and an actual speech of your soul to him, through Jesus Christ, for it is only God in Christ Jesus that is accessible at all. Going thus to God, we tell him that we are all wrong, and want to be set right; we tell him we wish to be reconciled to him, and are ashamed that we should have sinned against him; we then put our trust in his Son, and we are saved. O soul, go to God: it matters not though the prayer you come with may be a very broken prayer, or even if it has mistakes in it, as the prodigal's prayer had when he said, "Make me as one of thy hired servants;" the language of the prayer will not signify so long as you really approach to God. "Him that cometh to me," says Jesus, "I will in no wise cast out;" and Jesus ever liveth to make intercessions for them that come to God through him.

Here, then, is the great Protestant doctrine. The Romish doctrine says you must go round by the back door, and half-a-dozen of the Lord's servants must knock for you, and even then you may never be heard; but the grand old Protestant doctrine is, come to God yourself; come with no other mediator than Jesus Christ; come just as you are without merits and good works; trust in Jesus and your sins will be forgiven you.

There is my second point: there was action, and that action was contact with God.

III. Now, thirdly, IN THAT ACTION THERE WAS AN ENTIRE YIELDING UP OF HIMSELF. In the prodigal's case, his proud independence and self-will were gone. In other days he demanded his portion, and resolved to spend it as he pleased, but now he is willing to be as much under rule as a hired servant, he has had enough of being his own master, and is weary of the distance from God which self-will always creates. He longs to get into a child's true place, namely, that of dependence and loving submission. The great mischief of all was his distance from his father, and he now feels it to be so. His great thought is to remove that distance by humbly returning, for then he feels that all other ills will come to an end. He yields up his cherished freedom, his boasted independence, his liberty to think and do and say whatever he chose, and he longs to come under loving rule and wise guidance. Sinner, are you ready for this? If so, come and welcome; your father longs to press you to his bosom!

He gave up all idea of self-justification, for he said, "I have *sinned.*" Before he would have said, "I have a right to do as I like with my own; who is to dictate how I shall spend my own money. If I do sow a few wild oats, every young man does the same. I have been very generous, if nothing else; nobody can call me greedy. I am no hypocrite. Look at your canting Methodists, how they deceive people! There's nothing of that in me, I'll warrant you; I am an outspoken man of the world; and after all, a good deal better in disposition than my elder brother, fine fellow though he pretends to be." But now the prodigal boasts no longer. Not a syllable of self-praise falls from his lips; he mournfully confesses, "I have sinned against heaven and before thee." Sinner, if you would be saved you also must come down from your high places, and acknowledge your iniquity. Confess that you have done wrong, and do not try to extenuate your offence; do not offer apologies and make your case better than it is, but humbly plead guilty and leave your soul in Jesu's hands. Of two things, to sin or to deny the sin, probably to deny the sin is the worse of the two, and shows a blacker heart. Acknowledge your fault, man, and tell your heavenly Father that if it were not for his mercy you would have been in hell, and that as it is you richly deserve to be there even now. Make your case rather blacker than it is if you can; this I say because I know you cannot do any such thing. When a man is in the hospital it cannot be of any service to him to pretend to be better than he is; he will not receive any more medical attention on that account, but rather the other way, for the worse his case the more likely is the physician to give him special notice. Oh, sinner, lay bare before God thy sores, thy putrifying sores of sin, the horrid ulcers of thy deep depravity, and cry, "O Lord, have mercy upon me?" This is the way of wisdom. Have done with pride and self-righteousness, and make thy appeal to the undeserved pity of the Lord, and thou will speed.

Observe that the prodigal yielded up himself so thoroughly that he owned his father's love to him to be an aggravation of his guilt: so I take it he means when he says, "Father, I have sinned." It adds an emphasis to the "*I have sinned*" when it follows after the word "*father.*" "Thou good God, I have broken thy good laws; thou loving, tender, merciful God, I have done wrong wantonly and wickedly against thee. Thou hast been a very loving Father to me, and I have been a most ungenerous and shameless traitor to thee, rebelling without cause. I confess this frankly and humbly, and with many tears. Ah! hadst thou been a tyrant I might have gathered some apology from thy severity, but thou hast been a Father, and this makes it worse that I should sin against thee." It is sweet to hear such a confession as this poured out into the Father's bosom.

The penitent also yielded up all his supposed rights and claims upon his father, saying, "I am not worthy to be called thy son." He might have said, "I have sinned, but still I am thy child," and most of us would have thought it a very justifiable argument; but he does not say so, he is too humble for that, he owns, "I am no more worthy to be called thy son." A sinner is really broken down when he acknowledges that if God would have no mercy on him, but cast him away for for ever, it would be no more than justice.

> "Should sudden vengeance seize my breath,
> I must pronounce thee just in death;
> And, if my soul were sent to hell,
> Thy righteous law approves it well."

That soul is not far from peace which has ceased arguing and submits to the sentence. Oh, sinner, I urge thee, if thou wouldst find speedy rest, go and throw thyself at the foot of the cross where God meets such as thou art, and say, "Lord, here I am; do what thou wilt with me. Never a word of excuse will I offer, nor one single plea by way of extenuation. I am a mass of guilt and misery, but pity me, oh, pity me! No rights or claims have I; I have forfeited the rights of creatureship by becoming a rebel against thee. I am lost and utterly undone before the bar of thy justice. From that justice I flee and hide myself in the wounds of thy Son. According to the multitude of thy tender mercies, blot out my transgressions!"

Once again, here was such a yielding up of himself to his father that no terms or conditions are mentioned or implied. He begs to be received, but a servant's place is good enough for him; amongst the scullions of the kitchen he is content to take his place, so long as he may be forgiven. He does not ask for a little liberty to sin, or stipulate for a little self-righteousness wherein he may boast; he gives all up. He is willing to be anything or nothing, just as his father pleases, so that he may but be numbered with his household. No weapons of rebellion are in his hands now. No secret opposition to his father's rule lingers in his soul, he is completely subdued, and lies at his father's feet. Our Lord never crushed a soul yet that lay prostrate at his feet, and he never will. He will stoop down and say, "Rise, my child; rise, for I have forgiven thee. Go and sin no more. I have loved thee with an everlasting love." Come and let us return unto the Lord, for he hath torn, and he will heal us; he hath smitten, and he will bind us up. He will not break the bruised reed, nor quench the smoking flax.

IV. Notice further, and fourthly, that IN THIS ACT THERE WAS A MEASURE OF FAITH IN HIS FATHER—a measure, I say, meaning thereby not much faith, but some. A little faith saves the soul. There was faith in his father's power. He said, "In my father's house there is bread enough and to spare." Sinner, dost thou not believe that God is able to save thee; that through Jesus Christ he is able to supply thy soul's needs. Canst thou not get as far as this, "Lord, if thou wilt thou canst make me clean." The prodigal had also some faith in his father's readiness to pardon; for if he had not so hoped, he would never have returned to his father at all: if he had been sure that his father would never smile upon him he would never have returned to him. Sinner, do believe that God is merciful, for so he is. Believe, through Jesus Christ, that he willeth not the death of the sinner, but had rather that he should turn to him and live; for as surely as God liveth, this is truth, and do not thou believe a lie concerning thy God. The Lord is not hard or harsh, but he rejoices to pardon great transgressions. The prodigal also believed in his father's readiness to bless him. He felt sure that his father would go as far as propriety would permit, for he said, "I am not worthy to be called thy son, but make me at least thy servant." In this also he admitted that his father was so good, that even to be his servant would be a great matter. He was contented even to get the lowest place, so long as he might be under the shade of so good a protector.

Ah, poor sinner, dost thou not believe that God will have mercy on thee if he can do so consistently with his justice? If thou believest that, I have good news to tell thee. Jesus Christ, his Son, has offered such an atonement, that God can be just, and yet the justifier of him that believeth; he has mercy upon the vilest, and justifieth the ungodly, and accepteth the very chief of sinners through his dear Son. Oh, soul, have faith in the atonement. The atonement made by the personal sacrifice of the Son of God must be infinitely precious; believe thou that there is efficacy enough in it for thee. It is thy safety to fly to that atonement and cling to the Cross of Christ, and thou wilt honour God by so doing; is the only way in which thou canst honour him. Thou canst honour him by believing that he can save thee, even thee. The truest faith is that which believes in the mercy of God in the teeth of conscious unworthiness. The penitent in the parable went to his father too unworthy to be called his son, and yet he said, "My father." Faith has a way of seeing the blackness of sin, and yet believing that God can make the soul as white as snow. It is not faith that says, "I am a little sinner, and therefore God can forgive me;" but that is faith which cries, "I am a great sinner, an accursed and condemned sinner, and yet, for all that, God's infinite mercy can forgive me, and the blood of Christ can make me clean." Believe in the teeth of thy feelings, and in spite of thy conscience; believe in God, though everything within thee seems to say, "He cannot save thee; he will not save thee." Believe in God, sinner, over the tops of mountain sins. Do as John Bunyan says he did, for he was so afraid of his sins and of the punishment thereof, that he could not but run into God's arms, and he said, "Though he had held a drawn sword in his hands, I would have run on the very point of it, rather than have kept away from him." So do thou, poor sinner. Believe thy God. Believe in nothing else, but trust thy God, and thou wilt get the blessing. It is wonderful the power of faith over God, it binds his justice and constrains his grace. I do not know how to illustrate it better than by a little story. When I walked down my garden some time ago I found a dog amusing himself among the flowers. I knew that he was not a good gardener, and no dog of mine, so I threw a stick at him and bade him begone. After I had done so, he conquered me, and made me ashamed of having spoken roughly to him, for he picked up my stick, and, wagging his tail right pleasantly, he brought the stick to me, and dropped it at my feet. Do you think I could strike him or drive him away after that? No, I patted him and called him good names. The dog had conquered the man. And if you, poor sinner, dog as you are, can have confidence enough in God to come to him just as you are, it is not in his heart to spurn you. There is an omnipotence in simple faith which will conquer even the divine Being himself. Only do but trust him as he reveals himself in Jesus, and you shall find salvation.

V. I have not time or strength to dwell longer here, and so I must notice, fifthly, that THIS ACT OF COMING INTO CONTACT WITH GOD IS PERFORMED BY THE SINNER JUST AS HE IS. I do not know how wretched the prodigal's appearance may have been, but I will be bound to say he had grown none the sweeter by having fed swine, nor do I suppose his garments had been very sumptuously embroidered by gathering husks for them from the trees. Yet, just as he was, he came. Surely he might have spent an hour profitably in cleansing his flesh and his clothes. But no, he said, "I will arise," and no sooner said than done! he did arise, and he came to his father. Every moment that a sinner stops away from God in order to get better he is but adding to his sin, for the radical sin of all is his being away from God and the longer he stays in it the more he sins. The attempt to perform good works apart from God is like the effort of a thief to set his stolen goods in order, his sole duty is to return them at once. The very same pride which leads men away from God may be seen in their self-conceited notion that they can improve themselves while still they refuse to return to him. The essence of their fault is that they are far off from God, and whatever they do, so long as that distance remains, nothing is effectually done. I say the radical of the whole matter is distance from God, and therefore the commencement of setting matters right lies in arising and returning to him from whom they have departed.

The prodigal was bound to go home just as he was, for there was nothing that he could do. He was reduced to such extremities that he could not purchase a fresh piece of cloth to mend his garments, nor a farthing's worth of soap with which to cleanse his flesh; and it is a great mercy when a man is so spiritually reduced that he cannot do anything but go to his God as a beggar, when he is so bankrupt that he cannot pay a farthing in the pound, when he is so lost that he cannot even repent or believe apart from God, but feels that he is for ever undone unless the Lord shall interpose. It is our wisdom to go to God for everything.

Moreover, there was nothing needed from the prodigal but to return to his father. When a child who has done wrong comes back, the more its face is blurred with tears the better. When a beggar asks for charity, the more his clothes are in rags the better. Are not rags and sores the very livery of beggars? I once gave a man a pair of shoes because he said he was in need of them; but after he had put them on and gone a little way I overtook him in a gateway taking them off in order to go barefooted again. I think they were patent leather, and what should a beggar do in such attire? He was changing them for "old shoes and clouted," those were suitable to his business. A sinner is never so well arrayed for pleading as when he comes in rags. At his worst, the sinner, for making an appeal to mercy, is at his best. And so, sinners, there is no need for you to linger; come just as you are. "But must we not wait for the Holy Spirit?" Ah, beloved, he who is willing to arise and go to his Father has the Holy Spirit. It is the Holy Spirit who moves us to return to God, and it is the spirit of the flesh or of the devil that would bid us wait.

How now, sinners? Some of you are sitting in those pews; where are you? I cannot find you out, but my Master can, he has made this sermon on purpose for you. "Well, but I would like to get home and pray." Pray where you are, in the pew. "But I cannot speak out aloud." You may if you like, I won't stop you. "But I should not like." Well, don't, then. God can hear you without a sound, though I wish sometimes we did hear people cry out, "What must I do to be saved?" I would gladly hear the prayer, "God be merciful to me a sinner." But if men cannot hear you. the Lord can hear the cries of their hearts. Now, just sit still a minute, and say, "My God I must come to thee. Thou art in Jesus Christ, and in him thou has already come a great way to meet me. My soul wants thee; take me now, and make me what I ought to be. Forgive me, and accept me." It is the turning-point of a man's life when that is done, wherever it is, whether in a workshop, or in a saw-pit, in a church, or in a tabernacle; it does not matter where. There is the point—the getting to God in Christ, giving all up, and by faith resting in the mercy of God.

VI. The last point of all is this—THAT ACT WROUGHT THE GREATEST CONCEIVABLE CHANGE IN THE MAN. He was a new man after that. Harlots, winebibbers, you have lost your old companion now! He has gone to his Father, and his Father's company and yours will never agree. A man's return to his God means his leaving the chambers of vice and the tables of riot. You may depend upon it whenever you hear of a professing Christian living in uncleanness, he has not been living anywhere near his God. He may have talked a great deal about it, but God and unchastity never agree; if you have friendship with God you will have no fellowship with the unfruitful works of darkness.

Now, too, the penitent has done with all degrading works to support himself. You will not find him feeding swine any more, or making a swine of himself either by trusting in priests or sacraments; he will not confess to a priest again, or pay a penny to get his mother out of purgatory; he is not such a fool as that any more. He has been to his God on his own account, and he does not want any of these shavelings to go to God for him. He has got away from that bondage. No more pig-feeding; no more superstition for him! "Why," says he, "I have access with boldness to the mercy-seat, and what have I to do with the priests of Rome?"

There is a change in him in all ways. Now he has come to his father his pride is broken down. He no longer glories in that which he calls his own; all his glory is in his father's free pardoning love. He never boasts of what he has, for he owns that he has nothing but what his father gives him; and though he is far better off than ever he was in his spendthrift days, yet he is as unassuming as a little child. He is a gentleman-commoner upon the bounty of his God, and lives from day to day by a royal grant from the table of the King of kings. Pride is gone, but content fills its room. He would have been contented to be one of the servants of the house, much more satisfied is he to be a child. He loves his father with a new love; he cannot even mention his name without saying, "And he forgave me, he forgave me freely, he forgave me all, and he said, 'Bring forth the best robe and put it on him; put a ring on his hand and shoes on his feet.'" From the day of his restoration the prodigal is bound to his Father's home, and reckons it to be one of his greatest blessings that it is written in the covenant of grace, "I will put my fear in their hearts, that they shall not depart from me."

This morning I believe that God in his mercy means to call many sinners to himself. I am often very much surprised to find how the Lord guides my word according to the persons before me. Last Sunday there came here a young son of a gentleman, a foreigner, from a distant land, under considerable impressions as to the truth of the Christian religion. His father is a follower of one of the ancient religions of the East, and this young gentleman naturally felt it a great difficulty that he would probably make his father angry if he became a Christian. Judge, then, how closely the message of last Sabbath came home to him, when the text was, "What if thy father answer thee roughly?" He came to tell me that he thanked God for that message, and he hoped to bear up under the trial, should persecution arise. I feel that I am with equal plainness speaking to some of you. I know I am. You are saying, "May I now go to God just as I am, and through Jesus Christ yield myself up; and will he forgive me?" Dear brother, or dear sister, wherever you may be, *try it.* That is the best thing to do: *try it;* and, if the angels do not set the bells in heaven ringing, God has altered from what he was last week, for I know he received poor sinners then, and he will receive them now. The worst thing I dread about you is, lest you should say, "I will think of it." *Don't* think of it. *Do it!* Concerning this no more thinking is needed; but to do it. Get away to God. Is it not according to nature that the creature should be at peace with its Creator? Is it not according to your conscience? Is there not something within you which cries, "Go to God in Christ Jesus." In the case of that poor prodigal, the famine said to him, "Go home!" Bread was dear, meat was scarce, he was hungry, and every pang of want said, "Go home! Go home!" When he went to his old friend the citizen, and he asked him for help, his scowling looks said, "Why don't you go home?" There is a time with sinners when even their old companions seem to say, "We do not want you. You are too miserable and melancholy. Why don't you go home?" They sent him to feed swine, and the very hogs grunted, "Go home?" When he picked up those carob husks and tried to eat them, they crackled, "Go home." He looked upon his rags, and they gaped at him, "*Go home.*" His hungry belly and his faintness cried, "*Go home.*" Then he thought of his father's face, and how kindly it had looked at him, and it seemed to say, "Come home!" He remembered the bread enough and to spare, and every morsel seemed to say, "Come home!" He pictured the servants sitting down to dinner and feasting to the full, and every one of them seemed to look right away over the wilderness to him and to say, "Come home! Thy father feeds us well. Come home!" Everything said, "Come home!" Only the devil whispered, "Never go back. Fight it out! Better starve than yield! Die game!" But then he had got away from the devil this once, for he had come to himself, and he said, "No; I will arise and go to my father." Oh that you would be equally wise. Sinner, what is the use of being damned for the sake of a little pride. Yield thee, man! Down with thy pride! You will not find it so hard to submit if you remember that dear Father who loved us and gave himself for us in the person of his own dear Son. You will find it sweet to yield to such a friend. And when you get your head in his bosom, and feel his warm kisses on your cheek, you will soon feel that it is sweet to weep for sin—sweet to confess your wrong doing, and sweeter still to hear him say, "I have blotted out thy sins like a cloud, and like a thick cloud thy transgressions." "Though your sins be as scarlet, they shall be as white as snow; though they be red like crimson, they shall be as wool."

God Almighty grant this may be the case with hundreds of you this morning. He shall have all the glory of it, but my heart shall be very glad, for I feel nothing of the spirit of the elder brother within me, but the greatest conceivable joy at the thought of making merry with you by-and-by, when you come to own my Lord and Master, and we sit together at the sacramental feast, rejoicing in his love. God bless you, for his sake. Amen.

PORTION OF SCRIPTURE READ BEFORE SERMON—Luke xv.

Metropolitan Tabernacle Pulpit.

PRODIGAL LOVE FOR THE PRODIGAL SON.

A Sermon

INTENDED FOR READING ON LORD'S-DAY, DECEMBER 27TH, 1891,

DELIVERED BY

C. H. SPURGEON,

AT THE METROPOLITAN TABERNACLE, NEWINGTON,

On Lord's-day Evening, March 29th, 1891.

"And kissed him."—Luke xv. 20.

IN the Revised Version, if you will kindly look at the margin, you will find that the text there reads, "*And kissed him much.*" This is a very good translation of the Greek, which might bear the meaning, "Kissed him earnestly," or "Kissed him eagerly," or "Kissed him often." I prefer to have it in very plain language, and therefore adopt the marginal reading of the Revised Version, "Kissed him much," as the text of my sermon, the subject of which will be, the overflowing love of God toward the returning sinner.

The first word "and" links us on to all that had gone before. The parable is a very familiar one, yet it is so full of sacred meaning that it always has some fresh lesson for us. Let us, then, consider the preliminaries to this kissing. On the son's side there was something, and on the father's side much more. Before the prodigal son received these kisses of love, he had said in the far country, "I will arise and go to my father." He had, however, done more than that, else his father's kiss would never have been upon his cheek. The resolve had become a deed: "He arose, and came to his father." A bushelful of resolutions is of small value; a single grain of practice is worth the whole. The determination to return home is good; but it is when the wandering boy begins the business of really carrying out the good resolve, that he draws near the blessing. If any of you here present have long been saying, "I will repent; I will turn to God;" leave off resolving, and come to practising; and may God in his mercy lead you both to repent and to believe in Christ!

Before the kisses of love were given, this young man was on his way to his father; but he would not have reached him unless his father had come the major part of the way. When you give God an inch, he will give you an ell. If you come a little way to him, when you are "yet a great way off" he will run to meet you. I do not know that the prodigal saw his father, but his father saw him. The eyes of mercy are quicker than the eyes of repentance. Even the eye of our faith is dim compared with the eye of God's love. He sees a sinner long before a sinner sees him.

I do not suppose that the prodigal travelled very fast. I should imagine that he came very slowly—

> "With heavy heart and downcast eye,
> With many a sob and many a sigh."

He was resolved to come, yet he was half afraid. But we read that his father ran. Slow are the steps of repentance, but swift are the feet of forgiveness. God can run where we can scarcely limp, and if we are limping towards him, he will run towards us. These kisses were given in a hurry; the story is narrated in a way that almost makes us realize that such was the case: there is a sense of haste in the very wording of it. His father "ran, and fell on his neck, and kissed him;"—kissed him eagerly. He did not delay a moment; for though he was out of breath, he was not out of love. "He fell on his neck, and kissed him much." There stood his son ready to confess his sin; therefore did his father kiss him all the more. The more willing thou art to own thy sin, the more willing is God to forgive thee. When thou dost make a clean breast of it, God will soon make a clear record of it. He will wipe out the sin that thou dost willingly acknowledge and humbly confess before him. He that was willing to use his lips for confession, found that his father was willing to use his lips for kissing him.

See the contrast. There is the son, scarcely daring to think of embracing his father, yet his father has scarcely seen him before he has fallen on his neck. The condescension of God towards penitent sinners is very great. He seems to stoop from his throne of glory to fall upon the neck of a repentant sinner. God on the neck of a sinner! What a wonderful picture! Can you conceive it? I do not think you can; but if you cannot imagine it, I hope that you will realize it. When God's arm is about our neck, and his lips are on our cheek, kissing us much, then we understand more than preachers or books can ever tell us of his condescending love.

The father "saw" his son. There is a great deal in that word, "saw." He saw who it was; saw where he had come from; saw the swineherd's dress; saw the filth upon his hands and feet; saw his rags; saw his penitent look; saw what he had been; saw what he was; and saw what he would soon be. "His father saw him." God has a way of seeing men and women that you and I cannot understand. He sees right through us at a glance, as if we were made of glass; he sees all our past, present and future.

"When he was yet a great way off, his father saw him." It was not with icy eyes that the father looked on his returning son. Love leaped into them, and as he beheld him, he "had compassion on him;" that is, he felt for him. There was no anger in his heart towards his son; he had nothing but pity for his poor boy, who had got into such a pitiable condition. It was true that it was all his own fault, but that did not come before his father's mind. It was the state that he was in, his poverty, his degradation, that pale face of his so wan with hunger, that touched his father to the quick. And God has compassion on the woes and miseries of men. They may have brought their troubles on themselves, and they have indeed done so; but nevertheless God has compassion upon them. "It is of the Lord's mercies that we are not consumed, because his compassions fail not."

We read that the father "ran." The compassion of God is followed by swift movements. He is slow to anger, but he is quick to bless. He does not take any time to consider how he shall show his love to penitent prodigals; that was all done long ago in the eternal covenant. He has no need to prepare for their return to him; that was all done on Calvary. God comes flying in the greatness of his compassion to help every poor penitent soul.

"On cherub and on cherubim,
Full royally he rode;
And on the wings of mighty winds
Came flying all abroad."

And when he comes, he comes to kiss. Master Trapp says that, if we had read that the father had kicked his prodigal son, we should not have been very much astonished. Well, I should have been very greatly astonished, seeing that the father in the parable was to represent God. But still, his son deserved all the rough treatment that some heartless men might have given; and had the story been that of a selfish human father only, it might have been written that "as he was coming near, his father ran at him, and kicked him." There are such fathers in the world, who seem as if they cannot forgive. If he had kicked him, it would have been no more than he had deserved. But no, what is written in the Book stands true for all time, and for every sinner,—"He fell on his neck, and kissed him;" kissed him eagerly, kissed him much.

What does this much kissing mean? It signifies that, when sinners come to God, he gives them a loving reception, and a hearty welcome. If any one of you, while I am speaking, shall come to God, expecting mercy because of the great sacrifice of Christ, this shall be true of you as it has been true of many of us: "He kissed him much."

I. First, this much kissing means MUCH LOVE. It means much love truly *felt;* for God never gives an expression of love without feeling it in his infinite heart. God will never give a Judas-kiss, and betray those whom he embraces. There is no hypocrisy with God; he never kisses those for whom he has no love. Oh, how God loves sinners! You who repent, and come to him, will discover how greatly he loves you. There is no measuring the love he bears towards you. He has loved you from before the foundation of the world, and he will love you when time shall be no more. Oh, the immeasurable love of God to sinners who come and cast themselves upon his mercy!

This much kissing also means much love *manifested.* God's people do not always know the greatness of his love to them. Sometimes, however, it is shed abroad in our hearts by the Holy Ghost which is given unto us. Some of us know at times what it is to be almost too happy to live! The love of God has been so overpoweringly experienced by us on some occasions, that we have almost had to ask for a stay of the delight because we could not endure any more. If the glory had not been veiled a little, we should have died of excess of rapture, or happiness. Beloved, God has wondrous ways of opening his people's hearts to the manifestation of his grace. He can pour in, not now and then a drop of his love, but great and mighty streams. Madame Guyon used to speak of the torrents of love that come sweeping through the spirit, bearing all before them. The poor prodigal in the parable had so much love manifested to him, that he might have sung of the torrents of his father's affection. That is the way God receives those whom he saves, giving them not a meagre measure of grace, but manifesting an overflowing love.

This much kissing means, further, much love *perceived*. When his father kissed him much, the poor prodigal knew, if never before, that his father loved him. He had no doubt about it; he had a clear perception of it. It is very frequently the case that the first moment a sinner believes in Jesus, he gets this "much" love. God reveals it to him, and he perceives it and enjoys it at the very beginning. Think not that God always keeps the best wine to the last; he gives us some of the richest dainties of his table the first moment we sit there. I recollect the joy that I had when first I believed in Jesus; and, even now, in looking back upon it, the memory of it is as fresh as if it were but yesterday. Oh, I could not have believed that a mortal could be so happy after having been so long burdened, and so terribly cast down! I did but look to Jesus on the cross, and the crushing load was immediately gone; and the heart which could only sigh and cry by reason of its burden, began to leap and dance and sing for joy. I had found in Christ all that I wanted, and I rested in the love of God at once. So may it be with you also, if you will but return to God through Christ. It shall be said of you as of this prodigal, "The father saw him, and ran, and fell on his neck, and kissed him in much love."

II. Secondly, this much kissing meant MUCH FORGIVENESS. The prodigal had many sins to confess; but before he came to the details of them, his father had forgiven him. I love confession of sin after forgiveness. Some suppose that after we are forgiven we are never to confess; but, oh, beloved, it is then that we confess most truly, because we know the guilt of sin most really! Then do we plaintively sing—

"My sins, my sins, my Saviour,
How sad on thee they fall!
Seen through thy gentle patience,
I tenfold feel them all.
I know they are forgiven,
But still their pain to me
Is all the grief and anguish
They laid, my Lord, on thee."

To think that Christ should have washed me from my sins in his own blood, makes me feel my sin the more keenly, and confess it the more humbly before God. The picture of this prodigal is marvellously true to the experience of those who return to God. His father kissed him with the kiss of forgiveness; and yet, after that, the young man went on to say, "Father, I have sinned against heaven, and before thee, and am no more worthy to be called thy son." Do not hesitate, then, to acknowledge your sin to God, even though you know that in Christ it is all put away.

From this point of view, those kisses meant, first, "*Your sin is all gone*, and will never be mentioned any more. Come to my heart, my son! Thou hast grieved me sore, and angered me; but, as a thick clòud, I have blotted out thy transgressions, and as a cloud thy sins."

As the father looked upon him, and kissed him much, there probably came another kiss, which seemed to say, "*There is no soreness left:* I have not only forgiven, but I have forgotten too. It is all gone, clean gone. I will never accuse you of it any more. I will never love you any the less. I will never treat you as though you were still an unworthy and untrustworthy person." Probably at that there came another kiss; for do not forget that his father forgave him "and kissed him much," to show that the sin was all forgiven.

There stood the prodigal, overwhelmed by his father's goodness, yet remembering his past life. As he looked on himself, and thought, "I have these old rags on still, and I have just come from feeding the swine," I can imagine that his father would give him another kiss, as much as to say, "My boy, I do not recollect the past; I am so glad to see you that *I do not see any filth on you, or any rags* on you either. I am so delighted to have you with me once more that, as I would pick up a diamond out of the mire, and be glad to get the diamond again, so do I pick you up, you are so precious to me." This is the gracious and glorious way in which God treats those who return to him. As for their sin, he has put it away so that he will not remember it. He forgives like a God. Well may we adore and magnify his matchless mercy as we sing—

> "In wonder lost, with trembling joy
>   We take the pardon of our God;
> Pardon for crimes of deepest dye;
>   A pardon bought with Jesus' blood;
> Who is a pardoning God like thee?
> Or who has grace so rich and free?"

"Well," says one, "can such a wonderful change ever take place with me?" By the grace of God it may be experienced by every man who is willing to return to God. I pray God that it may happen now, and that you may get such assurance of it from the Word of God, by the power of his Holy Spirit, and from a sight of the precious blood of Christ shed for your redemption, that you may be able to say, "I understand it now; I see how he kisses all my sin away; and when it rises, he kisses it away again; and when I think of it with shame, he gives me another kiss; and when I blush all over at the remembrance of my evil deeds, he kisses me again and again, to assure me that I am fully and freely forgiven." Thus the many kisses from the prodigal's father combined to make his wayward son feel that his sin was indeed all gone. They revealed much love and much forgiveness.

III. These repeated kisses meant, next, FULL RESTORATION. The prodigal was going to say to his father, "Make me as one of thy hired servants." In the far country he had resolved to make that request, but his father, with a kiss, stopped him. By that kiss, his *sonship was owned;* by it the father said to the wretched wanderer, "You are my son." He gave him such a kiss as he would only give to his own son. I wonder how many here have ever given such a kiss to anyone. There sits one who knows something of such kisses as the prodigal received. That father's girl went astray, and, after years of sin, she came back worn out, to die at home. He received her, found her penitent, and gladly welcomed her to his house. Ah, my dear friend, you know something about such kisses as those! And you, good woman, whose boy ran away, you can understand something about these kisses, too. He left you, and you did not hear of him for years, and he went on in a very vicious course of life. When you did hear of him, it well-nigh broke your heart, and when he came back, you hardly knew him. Do you recollect how you took him in? You felt that you wished that he was the little boy you used to press to your bosom; but now he was grown up to be a big man and a great sinner, yet you gave him such a kiss, and repeated your welcome so often, that he will never forget it, nor will you forget it either. You can understand that this overwhelming greeting was like the father saying, "My boy, you are my son. Despite all that you have done, you belong to me; however far you have gone in vice and folly, I own you. You are bone of my bone, and flesh of my flesh." In this parable Christ would have you know, poor sinner, that God will own you, if you come to him confessing your sin through Jesus Christ. He will gladly receive you; for all things are ready against the day that you return.

> "Spread for thee the festal board,
> See with richest dainties stored,
> To thy Father's bosom pressed,
> Yet again a child confessed;
> Never from his house to roam,
> Come and welcome, sinner, come."

The father received his son with many kisses, and so proved that his *prayer was answered.* Indeed, his father heard his prayer before he offered it. He was going to say, "Father, I have sinned," and to ask for forgiveness; but he got the mercy, and a kiss to seal it, before the prayer was presented. This also shall be true of thee, O sinner, who art returning to thy God, through Jesus Christ! You shall be permitted to pray, and God will answer you. Hear it, poor, despairing sinner, whose prayer has seemed to be shut out from heaven! Come to your Father's bosom now, and he will hear your prayers; and, before many days are over, you shall have the clearest proofs that you are fully restored to the divine favour by answers to your intercessions that shall make you marvel at the Lord's loving-kindness to you.

Further than this, you shall have all your *privileges restored,* even as this wandering young man was put among the children when he returned. As you see him now in the father's house, where he was received with the many kisses, he wears a son's robe, the family ring is on his finger, and the shoes of the home are on his feet. He eats no longer swine's food, but children's bread. Even thus shall it be with you if you return to God. Though you look so foul and so vile, and really are even more defiled than you look; and though you smell so strongly of the hogs among which you have been living that some people's nostrils would turn up at you, your Father will not notice these marks of your occupation in the far country with all its horrible defilement. See how this father treats his boy. He kisses him, and kisses him again, because he knows his own child, and, recognizing him as his child, and feeling his fatherly heart yearning over him, he gives him kiss after kiss. He kisses him much, to make him know that he has full restoration.

In this repeated kissing we see, then, these three things: much love, much forgiveness, and full restoration.

IV. But these many kisses meant even more than this. They revealed his father's EXCEEDING JOY. The father's heart is overflowing with gladness, and he cannot restrain his delight. I think he must have shown his joy by *a repeated look.* I will tell you the way I think the father behaved towards his son who had been dead, but was alive again, who had been lost, but was found. Let me try to describe the scene. The father has kissed his son, and he bids him sit down; then he comes in front of him, and looks at him, and feels so happy that he says, "I must give you another kiss," then he walks away a minute; but he is back again before long, saying to himself, "Oh, I must give him another kiss!" He gives him another, for he is so happy. His heart beats fast; he feels very joyful; the old man would like the music to strike up; he wants to be at the dancing; but meanwhile he satisfies himself by a repeated look at his long-lost child. Oh, I believe that God looks at the sinner, and looks at him again, and keeps on looking at him, all the while delighting in the very sight of him, when he is truly repentant, and comes back to his Father's house.

The repeated kiss meant, also, *a repeated blessing*, for every time he put his arms round him, and kissed him, he kept saying, "Bless you; oh, bless you, my boy!" He felt that his son had brought a blessing to him by coming back, and he invoked fresh blessings upon his head. Oh, sinner! if you did but know how God would welcome you, and how he would look at you, and how he would bless you, surely you would at once repent, and come to his arms and heart, and find yourself happy in his love.

The many kisses meant, also, *repeated delight.* It is a very wonderful thing that it should be in the power of a sinner to make God glad. He is the happy God, the source and spring of all happiness; what can we add to his blessedness? And yet, speaking after the manner of men, God's highest joy lies in clasping his wilful Ephraims to his breast, when he has heard them bemoaning themselves, and has seen them arising and returning to their home. God grant that he may see that sight even now, and have delight because of sinners returning to himself! Yea, we believe it shall be even so, because of his presence with us, and because of the gracious working of the Holy Spirit. Surely that is the teaching of the prophet's words: "The Lord thy God in the midst of thee is mighty; he will save, he will rejoice over thee with joy; he will rest in his love, he will joy over thee with singing." Think of the eternal God singing, and remember that it is because a wandering sinner has returned to him that he sings. He joys in the return of the prodigal, and all heaven shares in his joy.

V. I have not got through my subject yet. As we take a fifth look, we find that these many kisses mean OVERFLOWING COMFORT. This poor young man, in his hungry, faint, and wretched state, having come a very long way, had not much heart in him. His hunger had taken all energy out of him, and he was so conscious of his guilt that he had hardly the courage to face his father; so his father gives him a kiss, as much as to say, "Come, boy, do not be cast down; I love you."

"Oh, *the past*, *the past*, my father!" he might moan, as he thought of his wasted years; but he had no sooner said that than he received another kiss, as if his father said, "Never mind the past; I have forgotten all about that." This is the Lord's way with his saved ones. Their past lies hidden under the blood of atonement. The Lord saith by his servant Jeremiah, "The iniquity of Israel shall be sought for, and there shall be none; and the sins of Judah, and they shall not be found: for I will pardon them whom I reserve."

But then, perhaps, the young man looked down on his foul garments, and said, "*The present*, my father, *the present*, what a dreadful state I am in!" And with another kiss would come the answer, "Never mind the present, my boy. I am content to have thee as thou art. I love thee." This, too, is God's word to those who are "accepted in the Beloved." In spite of all their vileness, they are pure and spotless in Christ, and God says of each one of them, "Since thou wast precious in my sight, thou hast been honourable, and I have loved thee. Therefore, though in thyself thou art unworthy, through my dear Son thou art welcome to my home."

"Oh, but," the boy might have said, "*the future*, my father, *the future!* What would you think if I should ever go astray again?" Then would come another holy kiss, and his father would say, "I will see to the future, my boy; I will make home so bright for you that you will never want to go away again." But God does more than that for us when we return to him. He not only surrounds us with tokens of his love, but he says concerning us, "They shall be my people, and I will be their God: and I will give them one heart, and one way, that they may fear me for ever, for the good of them, and of their children after them: and I will make an everlasting covenant with them, that I will not turn away from them, to do them good; but I will put my fear in their hearts, that they shall not depart from me." Furthermore, he says to each returning one, "A new heart also will I give you, and a new spirit will I put within you: and I will take away the stony heart out of your flesh, and I will give you an heart of flesh. And I will put my spirit within you, and cause you to walk in my statutes, and ye shall keep my judgments, and do them."

Whatever there was to trouble the son, the father gave him a kiss to set it all right; and, in like manner, our God has a love-token for every time of doubt and dismay which may come to his reconciled sons. Perhaps one whom I am addressing says, "Even though I confess my sin, and seek God's mercy, I shall still be in sore trouble, for through my sin, I have brought myself down to poverty." "There is a kiss for you," says the Lord: "Thy bread shall be given thee, and thy water shall be sure." "But I have even brought disease upon myself by sin," says another. "There is a kiss for you, for I am Jehovah-Rophi, the Lord that healeth thee, who forgiveth all thine iniquities, who healeth all thy diseases." "But I am dreadfully down at the heel," says another. The Lord gives you also a kiss, and says, "I will lift you up, and provide for all your needs. No good thing will I withhold from them that walk uprightly." All the promises in this Book belong to every repentant sinner, who returns to God believing in Jesus Christ, his Son.

The father of the prodigal kissed his son much, and thus made him feel happy there and then. Poor souls, when they come to Christ, are in a dreadful plight, and some of them hardly know where they are. I have known them talk a lot of nonsense in their despair, and say hard and wicked things of God in their dreadful doubt. The Lord gives no answer to all that, except a kiss, and then another kiss. Nothing puts the penitent so much at rest as the Lord's repeated assurance of his unchanging love. Such a one the Lord has often received, "and kissed him much," that he might fetch him up even from the horrible pit, and set his feet upon a rock, and establish his goings. The Lord grant that many whom I am addressing may understand what I am talking about!

VI. And now for our sixth head, though you will think I am getting to be like the old Puritans with these many heads. But I cannot help it, for these many kisses had many meanings: love, forgiveness, restoration, joy, and comfort were in them, and also STRONG ASSURANCE.

The father kissed his son much to make him quite certain that it was *all real*. The prodigal, in receiving these many kisses, might say to himself, "All this love must be true, for a little while ago I heard the hogs grunt, and now I hear nothing but the kisses from my dear father's lips." So his father gave him another kiss, for there was no way of convincing him that the first was real like repeating it; and if there lingered any doubt about the second, the father gave him yet a third. If, when the dream of old was doubled, the interpretation was sure, these repeated kisses left no room for doubt. The father renewed the tokens of his love that his son might be fully assured of its reality.

He did it that in the future it might *never be questioned*. Some of us were brought so low before we were converted, that God gave us an excess of joy when he saved us, that we might never forget it. Sometimes the devil says to me, "You are no child of God." I have long ago given up answering him, for I find that it is a waste of time to argue with such a crafty old liar as he is; he knows too much for me. But if I must answer him, I say, "Why, I remember when I was saved by the Lord! I never can forget even the very spot of ground where first I saw my Saviour; there and then my joy rolled in like some great Atlantic billow, and burst in mighty foam of bliss, covering all things. I cannot forget it." That is an argument which even the devil cannot answer, for he cannot make me believe that such a thing never happened. The Father kissed me much, and I remember it full well. The Lord gives to some of us such a clear deliverance, such a bright, sunshiny day at our conversion, that henceforth we cannot question our state before him, but must believe that we are eternally saved.

The father put the assurance of this poor returning prodigal beyond all doubt. If the first kisses were given privately, when only the father and son were present, it is quite certain that, afterwards, he kissed him *before men*, where others could see him. He kissed him much in the presence of the household, that they also might not be calling in question that he was his father's child. It was a pity that the elder brother was not there also. You see he was away in the field. He was more interested in the crops than in the reception of his brother. I have known such a one in modern days. He was a man who did not come out to week-evening services. He was such a man of business that he did not come out on a Thursday night, and the prodigal came home at such a time, and so the elder brother did not see the father receive him. If he lived now, he would probably not come to the church-meetings; he would be too busy. So he would not get to know about the reception of penitent sinners. But the father, when he received that son of his, intended all to know, once for all, that he was indeed his child. Oh, that you might get these many kisses even now! If they are given to you, you will have, for the rest of your life, strong assurance derived from the happiness of your first days.

VII. I have done when I have said that I think that here we have a specimen of the INTIMATE COMMUNION which the Lord often gives to sinners when first they come to him. "His father saw him, and had compassion, and ran, and fell on his neck, and kissed him much."

You see, this was *before the family fellowship*. Before the servants had prepared the meal, before there had been any music or dancing in the family, his father kissed him. He would have cared little for all their songs, and have valued but slightly his reception by the servants, if, first of all, he had not been welcomed to his father's heart. So is it with us; we need first to have fellowship with God before we think much of union with his people. Before I go to join a church, I want my Father's kiss. Before the pastor gives me the right hand of fellowship, I want my heavenly Father's right hand to welcome me. Before I become recognized by God's people here below, I want a private recognition from the great Father above; and that he gives to all who come to him as the prodigal came to his father. May he give it to some of you now!

This kissing, also, was *before the table communion*. You know that the prodigal was afterwards to sit at his father's table, and to eat of the fatted calf; but before that, his father kissed him. He would scarcely have been able to sit easily at the feast without the previous kisses of love. The table communion, to which we are invited, is very sweet. To eat the flesh and drink the blood of Christ, in symbol, in the ordinance of the Lord's Supper, is, indeed, a blessed thing; but I want to have communion with God by the way of the love-kiss before I come there. "Let him kiss me with the kisses of his mouth." This is something private, ravishing, and sweet. God give it to many of you!

May you get the many kisses of your Father's mouth before you come into the church, or to the communion table!

These many kisses likewise came *before the public rejoicing.* The friends and neighbours were invited to share in the feast. But think how shamefaced the son would have been in their presence, if, first of all, he had not found a place in his father's love, or had not been quite sure of it. He would almost have been inclined to run away again. But the father had kissed him much, and so he could meet the curious gaze of old friends with a smiling face, until any unkind remarks they might have thought of making died away, killed by his evident joy in his father. It is a hard thing for a man to confess Christ if he has not had an overwhelming sense of communion with him. But when we are lifted to the skies in the rapture God gives to us, it becomes easy, not only to face the world, but to win the sympathy of even those who might have opposed themselves. This is why young converts are frequently used to lead others into the light; the Lord's many kisses of forgiveness have so recently been given to them, that their words catch the fragrance of divine love as they pass the lips just touched by the Lord. Alas, that any should ever lose their first love, and forget the many kisses they have received from their heavenly Father!

Lastly, all this was given *before the meeting with the elder brother.* If the prodigal son had known what the elder brother thought and said, I should not have wondered at all if he had run off, and never come back at all. He might have come near home, and then, hearing what his brother said, have stolen away again. Yes, but before that could happen, his father had given him the many kisses. Poor sinner! you have come in here, and perhaps you have found the Saviour. It may be that you will go and speak to some Christian man, and he will be afraid to say much to you. I do not wonder that he should doubt you, for you are not, in yourself, as yet a particularly nice sort of person to talk to. But, if you get your Father's many kisses, you will not mind your elder brother being a little hard upon you. Occasionally I hear of one, who wished to join the church, saying, "I came to see the elders, and one of them was rather rough with me. I shall never come again." What a stupid man you must be! Is it not their duty to be a little rough with some of you, lest you should deceive yourselves, and be mistaken about your true state? We desire lovingly to bring you to Christ, and if we are afraid that you really have not yet come back to God, with penitence and faith, should we not tell you so, like honest men? But suppose that you have really come, and your brother is mistaken; go and get a kiss from your Father, and never mind your brother. He may remind you how you have squandered your living, painting the picture even blacker than it ought to be; but your Father's kisses will make you forget your brother's frowns. If you think that in the household of faith you will find everybody amiable, and everyone willing to help you, you will be greatly mistaken. Young Christians are often frightened when they come across some who, from frequent disappointment of their hopes, or from a natural spirit of caution, or perhaps from a lack of spiritual life, receive but coldly those upon whom the Father has lavished much love. If that is your case, never mind these cross-grained elder brethren; get another kiss from your Father. Perhaps the reason it is written, "He kissed him *much*," was because the elder brother, when he came near him, would treat him so coldly, and so angrily refuse to join in the feast.

Lord, give to many poor trembling souls the will to come to thee! Bring many sinners to thy blessed feet, and while they are yet a great way off, run and meet them; fall on their neck, give them many kisses of love, and fill them to the full with heavenly delight, for Jesus Christ's sake! Amen.

PORTION OF SCRIPTURE READ BEFORE SERMON—Luke xv.

HYMNS FROM "OUR OWN HYMN BOOK"—568, 521, 548.

Metropolitan Tabernacle Pulpit.

THE RECEPTION OF SINNERS.

A Sermon

DELIVERED ON LORD'S-DAY MORNING, NOVEMBER 22ND, 1874, BY

C. H. SPURGEON,

AT THE METROPOLITAN TABERNACLE, NEWINGTON.

"But the father said to his servants, Bring forth the best robe, and put it on him; and put a ring on his hand, and shoes on his feet: And bring hither the fatted calf, and kill it; and let us eat and be merry."—Luke xv. 22, 23.

LAST Lord's-day we spoke upon the consecration of priests. That theme might seem too high for troubled hearts and trembling consciences, who fear that they shall never be made priests and kings unto God. So glorious a privilege appears to them to hang in the dim, distant future, if, indeed, they reach it at all. Therefore, at this time, we will go down from the elevated regions to comfort those who are seeking the Lord, with the view of helping them in their turn to climb also.

We speak this morning, not of the consecration of priests, but of the reception of sinners, and this, according to our text, is a very joyful business, it is even described as a merrymaking, accompanied with music and with dancing. We very frequently speak of the sorrow for sin which accompanies conversion, and I do not think we can speak of it too often; but yet there is a possibility of our overlooking the equally holy and remarkable joy which attends the return of a soul to God. It has been a very common error to suppose that a man must pass through a very considerable time of despondency, if not of horror of mind, before he can find peace with God: now in this parable the father seems determined to cut short that period; he stops his son in the very middle of his confession, and before he can ask to be made as one of the hired servants, his mournful style is changed for rejoicing, for the father has already fallen on his neck and kissed his trembling lips into a sweet silence. It is not the Lord's desire that sinners should tarry long in the state of unbelieving conviction of sin, it is something wrong in themselves which keeps them there; either they are ignorant of the freeness and fulness of Christ, or they harbour self-righteous hopes, or they cling to their sins. Sin lieth at the door, it is no work of God which blocks the way. He delights in their delight, and joys in their joy. It is the Father's will that the penitent sinner should at once believe in Jesus, at once find complete forgiveness, and immediately enter into rest. If any of you came to Jesus without the dreary interval of terror which is so frequent, I pray you do not judge yourselves as though your conversions were dubious—they are all the more instead of all the less genuine because they bear rather the marks of the gospel than of the law. The weeping of Peter, which in a few days turns to joy, is far better than the horror of Judas, which ends in suicide. Conversions, as recorded in Scripture, are for the most part exceedingly rapid. They were pricked in the heart at Pentecost, and the same day they were baptised and added to the church, because they had found peace with God through Jesus Christ. Paul was smitten down with conviction, and in three days was a baptised believer. Perhaps the figure is inapt, but I was about to say that sometimes God's power is so very near us that the lightning flash of conviction is often attended at the very same moment by the deep thunder of the Lord's voice, which drives away our fears and proclaims peace and pardon to the soul. In many cases the sharp needle of the law is immediately followed by the silken thread of the gospel; the showers of repentance are succeeded at once by the sunshine of faith; peace overtakes penitence, and walks arm in arm with her into yet fuller rest.

Having thus reminded you that God would have penitents very soon rejoice, I want to spend this morning in setting forth the joy which is caused by pardoned sin. That joy is threefold. We will talk about it, first, as *the joy of God over sinners;* secondly, *the joy of sinners in God;* and, thirdly, what is so often forgotten, *the joy of the servants,* for they too rejoiced, for the father said, "Let *us* eat and be merry;" and one of the points of the parable is just this, that as in the case of the lost sheep the shepherd calleth together his friends and neighbours, and as in the case of the piece of money the woman calleth her neighbours together, so in this case, also, others share in the joy which chiefly belongs to the loving father and the returning wanderer.

I. THE JOY OF GOD OVER SINNERS. It is always difficult to speak of the ever-blessed God becomingly when we have to describe him as touched by emotions; I pray, therefore, to be guided in my speech by the Holy Spirit. We have been educated into the idea that the Lord is above emotions, either of sorrow or pleasure. That he cannot suffer, for instance, is always laid down as a self-evident postulate. Is that quite so clear? Cannot he do or bear anything he chooses to do? What means the Scripture which says that man's sin before the flood made the Lord repent that he had made man on the earth, "and it grieved him at his heart"? Is there no meaning in the Lord's own language, "Forty years long was I grieved with this generation"? Are we not forbidden to grieve the Holy Spirit? Is he not described as having been vexed by ungodly men! Surely, then, he can be grieved: it cannot be an altogether meaningless expression. For my part, I rejoice to worship the living God, who, because he is living, does grieve and rejoice. It makes one feel more love to him than if he dwelt on some serene Olympus, careless of all our woes, because incapable of any concern about us, or interest in us, one way or the other. To look upon him as utterly impassive and incapable of anything like emotion does not, to my mind, exalt the Lord, but rather brings him down to be comparable to the gods of stone or wood, which cannot sympathise with their worshippers. No, Jehovah is not insensible. He is the living God, and everything that goes with life,—pure, perfect, holy life, is to be found in him. Yet must such a subject always be spoken of very tenderly, with solemn awe, because, albeit we know something of what God is, for we are made in the image of God, and the best likeness of God undoubtedly was man as he came from his Maker's hand, yet man is not God, and even in his perfectness he must have been a very tiny miniature of God; while now that he has sinned he has blotted and blurred that image. The finite cannot fully mirror the Infinite, nor can the grand, glorious, essential properties of Deity be communicated to creatures: they must remain peculiar to God alone. The Lord is, however, continually represented as displaying joy. Moses declared to sinful Israel, that if they returned and obeyed the voice of the Lord, the Lord would again rejoice over them for good, as he rejoiced over their fathers (Deut. xxx. 9). The Lord is said to rejoice in his works and to delight in mercy, and surely we must believe it. Wherefore should we doubt it? Many passages of Scripture speak very impressively of God's joy in his people. Zephaniah puts it in the strongest manner: "He will save, he will rejoice over thee with joy; he will rest in his love, he will joy over thee with singing." Our God is for ever the happy or blessed God; we cannot think of him as other than supremely blessed. Still, from the Scriptures we gather that he displays on certain occasions a special joy which he would have us recognise. I do not think that it can be mere parable, but it is real fact, that the Lord does rejoice over returning and repenting sinners.

Every being manifests its joy according to its nature, and seeks means for its display suitable to itself. It is so with men. When the old Romans celebrated a triumph because some great general returned a victor from Africa, Greece, or Asia with the spoils of a long campaign, how did the fierce Roman nature express its joy? Why, in the Colosseum, or in some yet vaster amphitheatre, where buzzing nations choked the ways, they gathered in their myriads to behold not only beasts, but their fellow men, "butchered to make a Roman holiday." Cruelty upon an extraordinary scale was their way of expressing the joy of their iron hearts. Look at the self-indulgent man! He has had a prosperous season, and has made a lucky hit, as he calls it, or some event has occurred in his family which makes him very jubilant; what will he do to show forth his joy? Will he bow the knee in gratitude, or lift a hymn of praise? Not he. He will hold a drinking bout, and when he and his fellows are mad with wine his joy will find expression! The sensual show their joy by sensuality. Now, God whose name is good, and whose nature is love, when he has joy expresses it in mercy, in lovingkindness, and grace. The father's joy in the parable before us showed itself in the full forgiveness accorded, in the kiss of perfect love bestowed, in the gift of the best robe, the ring, and the sandals, and in the gladsome festival which filled the whole house with hallowed mirth. Everything expresses its joy according to its nature; infinite love, therefore, reveals its joy in acts of love.

The nature of God being as much above ours as the heaven is above the earth, the expression of his joy is therefore all the loftier, and his gifts the greater. Still, there is a likeness between God's way of expressing joy and ours, which it will be profitable to note. How do we express ourselves, ordinarily, when we are glad? We do so very commonly by a display of *bounty*. When in the olden time our kings came into the city of London, or a great victory was celebrated, the conduit in Cheapside ran with red wine, and even the gutters flowed with it. Then were there tables set in the street, and my lords, and the aldermen, and the mayor kept open house, and everybody was fed to the full. Joy was expressed by hospitality. You have seen the picture of the young heir coming of age, and have noticed how the artist depicts the great yard of the manor-house as full of men and women, who are eating and drinking to their hearts' content. At Christmas seasons, and upon marriage days and harvest homes, men ordinarily express their joy by bountiful provision; so also does the father in this wondrous parable exhibit the utmost bounty, representing thereby the boundless liberality of the great Father of spirits, who shows his joy over penitents by the manner in which he entertains them. The best robe, the ring, the shoes, and the fatted calf, and the "Let us eat and be merry," all show by their bountifulness that God is glad. His oxen and his fatlings are killed, for the feast of mercy is the banquet of the Lord. So unrivalled are the gifts of his gracious hand that the receivers of his favours have cried out in amazement, "Who is a God like unto thee!" Beloved, consider awhile the Lord's bounty to returning sinners, blotting out their sins like a cloud, and like a thick cloud their iniquities, justifying them in the righteousness of Christ, endowing them with his Holy Spirit, regenerating them, comforting them, illuminating them, purifying them, strengthening them, guiding them, protecting them, filling them with all his own fulness, satisfying their mouth with good things, and crowning them with tender mercies. I see in the bounty of God with which he so liberally endows returning sinners a mighty proof that his inmost soul rejoices over the salvation of men.

At glad times men generally manifest some *speciality* in their bounty. On the day of the young heir's coming of age the long stored cask of wine is broached, and the best bullock is roasted whole. So here in the parable we read, "*Bring forth* the best robe," indicating that it had been laid by and kept in store until then. Nobody had used that robe, it was locked up in the wardrobe, only to be brought out on some very special occasion. This was the happiest day that ever had made glad the house, and therefore "Bring forth the best robe," no other will suffice. Meat is wanted for the banquet. Let a calf be killed. Which shall it be? A calf taken at random from the herd? No, but *the fatted* calf which has been standing in the stalls, and is well fed, and has been reserved for a festival. Oh, beloved, when God blesses a sinner he shows his joy by giving him the reserved mercies, the *special* treasures of everlasting love, the precious things of grace, the secret of the covenant: yea, he has given to sinners the best of the best in giving them Christ Jesus, and the indwelling of the Holy Spirit. The best that heaven affords God bestows on sinners when they come to him. No scraps and odds and ends are dealt out to hungry and thirsty seekers, but in princely munificence of unstinting love the heavenly Father deals out abundant grace. I would that sinners would come and try my Lord's hospitality; they would find his table to be more richly loaded than even that of Solomon, though thirty oxen and a hundred sheep did not suffice for one day's provision for the household of that magnificent sovereign. If they would but come, even the largest-hearted among them would be wonder-struck as they saw how richly God supplied all their need, according to his riches in glory by Christ Jesus.

"Rags exchanged for costly treasure,
Shoes and ring and heaven's best robe!
Gifts of *love* which knows no measure;
Who can tell the heart of God?
All his loved ones—his redeemed ones,
Perfect are in his abode."

We also show our joy by a *concentration of thought* upon the object of it. When a man is carried away with joy he forgets everything else, and gives himself up to the one delight. David was so glad to bring back the Ark of the Lord that he danced before the Lord with all his might, being clad only with a linen ephod. He laid aside his stately garments, and thought so little of his dignity that Michal sneered at him ; he was so much absorbed in adoring his Lord that all regard to appearances was quite gone. Observe well the parable, and think you hear the father say, "Bring forth the best robe and put it on *him*, and put a ring on *his* hand and shoes on *his* feet, and let us eat and be merry, for *this my son* was dead and is alive again." The son alone is in the father's eye, and the whole house must be ordered in reference to him. Nothing is to be thought of to-day but the long-lost son, he is paramount in the wardrobe, the jewel room, the farmyard, the kitchen, and the banquetting chamber. He that was lost, he that was dead, he being found and alive, engrosses the whole of the father's mind. Sinner, it is wonderful how God sets all his thoughts on you according to his promise, "I will set mine eyes upon them for good," (Jer. xxiii. 6); and again, "I will watch over them to build and to plant saith the Lord." The Lord thinketh upon the poor and needy, his eyes are upon them and his ears are open to their cry. He thinks as much of each penitent sinner as if he were the only being in the universe. O penitent, for you is the working of the Lord's providence to bring you home, for you the training of his ministers that they might know how to reach your heart, for you the gifts of the Spirit upon them that they might be powerful with your conscience; yea, for you his Son, his eternal Son once bleeding on the cross, and now sitting in the highest heavens making intercession for you. I saw in Amsterdam the diamond cutting, and I noticed great wheels, a large factory and powerful engines, and all the power was made to bear upon a small stone no larger than the nail of my little finger. All that huge machinery for that little stone, because it was so precious! Methinks I see you poor insignificant sinners, who have rebelled against your God, brought back to your Father's house, and now the whole universe is full of wheels and all those wheels are working together for your good, to make out of you a jewel fit to glisten in the Redeemer's crown. God is not represented as saying more of creation than that "it was very good," but in the work of grace he is described as singing for joy. He breaks the eternal silence and cries, "my son is found." As the philosopher when he had compelled nature to yield her secret ran through the street crying, "Eureka! Eureka! I have found it! I have found it!" so does the Father dwell on the word, "my son that was dead, is alive again, he that was lost is found." The whole of Scripture aims at the bringing back again of the Lord's banished, for this the Redeemer leaves his glory, for this the church sweeps her house and lights her candle, and when the work is done all other bliss is secondary to the surpassing joy of the Lord, of which he bids his ransomed ones partake, saying, "Enter ye into the joy of your Lord."

We also show our joy by *an alacrity of motion.* I quoted David just now. It was so with him, he danced before the ark. I cannot imagine David walking slowly before the ark, or creeping after it like a mourner at a funeral. I often notice the difference between your coming to this place and people going to other places of worship. I remark a very solemn, stately, and sombre motion in almost everybody else, but you come tripping along as if you were glad to go up to the house of the Lord; you do not regard the place of our joyous assemblies as a sort of religious prison, but as the palace and banquetting house of the great King. When any one is joyous he is sure to show it by the quickness of his motions. Hearken to the father, he says, "Bring forth the best robe and put it on him, and put a ring on his hand, and shoes on his feet, and bring hither the fatted calf, and let us eat and be merry." As quickly as possible he pours out sentence after sentence. There is no delay; no interval between the commands. Might he not have said, "Bring forth the best robe and put it on him, and let us look at him awhile, and sit down and prepare him for the next step; and in an hour's time, or to-morrow, we will put a ring on his hand; and then soon we will put shoes on his feet; he is best without shoes for the present, for perhaps if he has shoes on he will run away. As to the festival, perhaps we had better rejoice over him when we see whether his repentance is genuine." No, no, no, the father's heart is too glad; he must bless his boy at once, heap on his favours, and multiply his tokens of love. When the Lord receives a sinner, he runs to meet him, he falls on his neck, he kisses him, he speaks to him, he forgives him, he justifies him, he sanctifies him, he puts him among the children, he opens the treasures of his grace to him, and all in quick succession. Within a few minutes after he has been cleansed from sin, the prodigal is robed, and adorned, and shod for service. The love of our Redeemer's heart made him say to the poor thief, "To-day shalt thou be with me in Paradise;" he would not let him linger in pain on the cross, but carried him away to Paradise in an hour or two. Love and joy are ever quick of foot. God is slow to anger, but he is so plenteous in his mercy that his grace overflows and rushes on like a torrent when it leaps along the ravine.

Once more, the joy of the father was shown as ours often is by *open utterance*. It is hard for a glad man to hold his tongue. What can dumb people do when they are very happy? I cannot imagine how they endure silence at such times; it must then be a terrible misfortune. When you are very happy you must tell somebody. So does this father. He pours out his joy, and the utterance is very simple. "My son was dead, and is alive again, was lost, and is found." Yet, simple as it is, it is poetry. The poetry of the Hebrews consisted in parallelism, or a repetition of the sense or a part of the words. Here are two lines which pair with each other, and make a verse of Hebrew poetry. Glad men when they speak naturally and simply always say the right thing in the very best manner, using nature's poetry, as does the father here. Note, also, that there is reiteration in his utterance. He might have been satisfied to say, "This my son was dead and is alive again." No; the fact is so sweet he must repeat it, "He was lost, and is found." Even thus we speak when we are very full of sweet content; the heart bubbleth up with a good matter, and over again and over again we rehearse our joy. When the morsel is sweet we roll it under the tongue. We cannot help it. So the Lord rejoices over sinners, and tells his joy in holy scripture in varied phrase and metaphor, and though those scriptures are simple in their style, yet they contain the very essence of poetry. The bards of the Bible stand in the first rank amongst the sons of song, God himself deigning to use poetry to utter his joy because a more prosaic manner would be all too cold and tame. Hear how he puts it: "As the bridegroom rejoiceth over the bride, so shall thy God rejoice over thee." "I will rejoice in Jerusalem and joy in my people." We might have been left in the dark about this joy of God; we might have been coldly informed that God would save sinners, and we might never have known that he found such joy in it; but the divine joy was too great to be concealed, the great heart of God could not restrain itself, he must tell out to all the universe the delight which the exercise of mercy brought to him. It was meet that he should make merry and be glad, and therefore he did it, for nothing that is meet to be done will ever be neglected by the Lord our God.

Thus, dear friends, have I feebly spoken of the joy of God, and I want you to notice that it is a delight in which every attribute of God takes a share. Condescension ran to meet the son, love fell on his neck, grace kissed him, wisdom clothed him, truth gave him the ring, peace shod him, wisdom provided the feast, and power prepared it. No one attribute of the divine nature quarrels with the forgiveness and salvation of a sinner; not one attribute holds back from the beloved employ. Power strengthens the weak, and mercy binds up the wounded; justice smiles upon the justified sinner, for it is satisfied through the atoning blood, and truth puts forth her hand to guarantee that the promise of grace is fulfilled; immutability confirms what has been done, and omniscience looks around to see that nothing is left undone. The whole of Deity is brought to bear upon a poor worm of the dust, to lift it up and transform it into an heir of God, joint-heir with the Only Begotten. The joy of God occupies the whole of his being, so that when we think of it we may well say, "Bless the Lord, O my soul, and all that is within me bless his holy name," since all that is within him is engaged to bless his saints.

This joy of the Lord should give every sinner great confidence in coming to God by Jesus Christ, for if you would be glad to be saved, he will be glad to save you; if you long to lay your head in your Father's bosom, your Father's bosom longs to have it there; if you pant to say, "I have sinned," he equally longs to say to you, by acts of love, "I forgive thee freely." If you pine to be his child in his own house once more, the door is open, and he himself is on the watch. Come and welcome, come and welcome, and no more delay.

II. I have now to speak of THE JOY OF THE SINNER. The son was glad. He did not express it in words, as far as I can see in the parable, but he felt it none the less—but all the more. Sometimes silence is discreet, and it was so in this case; at other times it is absolutely forced upon you by inability to utter the emotion, and this also was true of the prodigal. The son's heart was too full for utterance in words, but he had speaking eyes, and a speaking countenance as he looked on that dear father. As he put on the robe, the ring, and the shoes, he must have been too astonished to speak. He wept in showers that day, but the tears were not salt with grief; they were sweet tears, glittering like the dew of the morning. What would make the son glad, think you? Why, the father's love, the father's forgiveness, and restoration to his old place in the father's heart. That was the point. But then each gift would serve as a token of that love and make the joy overflow. There was *the robe* put on,—the dress of a son, and of a son well beloved and accepted. Have you noticed how the robe answered to his confession? The sentences match each other thus: "Father, I have sinned;"—"Bring forth the best robe and put it on him." Cover all his sins with Christ's righteousness; put away his sin by imputing to him the righteousness of the Lord Jesus. The robe also met his condition; he was in rags, therefore, "Bring forth the best robe and put it on him," and you shall see no more of his rags. It was fit that he should be thus arrayed, in token of his restoration. He who is re-endowed with the privileges of a son should not be dressed in sordid clothes, but wear raiment suitable to his station. Moreover, as a festival was about to begin he ought to wear a festive garment. It would not be seemly for him to feast and be merry in his rags. Put the best robe on him that he may be ready to take his place at the banquet. So when the penitent comes to God he is not only covered, as to the past, by the righteousness of Christ, but he is prepared for the future blessedness which is reserved for the pardoned ones, yea, he is fitted to begin the rejoicing at once.

Then came *the ring*, a luxury rather than a necessary, except that now he was a son it was well that he should be restored to all the honours of his relationship. The signet ring in the east in former times conferred great privileges: in those days men did not sign their names, but stamped with their signet upon wax, so that the ring gave a man power over property, and made him a sort of other self to the man whose ring he wore. The father gives the son a ring, and how complete an answer was that gift to another clause of his confession. Let me read the two sentences together, "I am no more worthy to be called thy son." "Put a ring on his hand." The gift precisely meets the confession. It also tallied with his changed condition. How singular that the very hand which had been feeding swine should now wear a ring. There were no rings on his hands when they were soiled at the trough, I warrant you; but now he is a swine-feeder no longer, but an honoured son of a rich father. Slaves wear no rings. Juvenal laughs at certain freed-men because they were seen walking up and down the Via Sacra with conspicuous rings on their fingers, the emblems of their new-found liberty. The ring indicated the penitent's liberty from sin, and his enjoyment of the full privileges of his Father's house. O, beloved, the Lord will make you glad if you come to him, by putting the seal of the Holy Spirit's indwelling upon you, which is both the earnest of the inheritance and the best adornment of the hand of your practical character. You shall have a sure and honourable token, and shall know that all things are yours, whether things present, or things to come. This ring upon your finger will declare your marriage union to Christ, set forth the eternal love which the Father has fixed upon you, and be the abiding pledge of the perfect work of the Holy Ghost.

Then they put *shoes* on his feet. I suppose he had worn out his own. In the east servants do not usually wear shoes at home, and especially in the best rooms of the house. The master and the son wear the sandals, but not the servants, so that this order was an answer to the last part of the penitent's prayer, "Make me as one of thy hired servants." "No," says the father, "put shoes on his feet." In the forgiven sinner the awe which puts off its shoes is to be overmatched by the familiarity which wears the shoes which infinite love provides. The forgiven one is no longer to tremble at Sinai, but he is to come unto Mount Zion, and to have familiar intercourse with God. Thus also the restored one was shod for filial service—he could run upon his father's errands, or work in his father's fields. He had now in every way all that he could want—the robe that covered him, the ring that adorned him, and the shoe that prepared him for travel or labour.

Now ye awakened and anxious ones who are longing to draw nigh to God, I would that this description of the joy of the prodigal would induce you to come at once. Come, ye naked, and he will say, "Bring forth the best robe." Come, ye that see your natural deformity through sin, and he will adorn you with a ring of beauty. Come, ye who feel as if you could not come, for ye have bleeding, weary feet, and he will shoe you with the silver sandals of his grace. Only do but come, and you shall have such joy in your hearts as you have never dreamed of. There shall be a young heaven born within your spirit, which shall grow and increase until it comes to the fulness of bliss.

III. The time has now come for us to dwell upon THE JOY OF THE SERVANTS. They were to be merry, and they were merry, for the music and the dancing which were heard outside could not have proceeded from one person only, there must have been many to join in it, and who should these be but the servants to whom the father gave his commands? They ate, they drank, they danced, they joined in the music. There are many of us here who are the servants of our own heavenly Father; though we are his children, we delight to be his servants. Now, whenever a sinner is saved, we have our share of joy. We have joy, first, *in the Father's joy*. They were so glad, because their lord was glad—good servants are always pleased when they see that their master is greatly gratified, and I am sure the Lord's servants are always joyous when they feel that their Lord is well pleased. That servant who went out to the elder brother, showed by his language that he was in sympathy with the father, for he pleaded with the son upon the matter; and when you are in sympathy with God, my dear brother or sister, if the Lord lets you see poor sinners saved you must and will rejoice with him. It will be to you better than finding a purse full of money, or making a great gain in business; yea, nothing in the world can give you more delight than to see some brother of yours or some child of yours made to rejoice in Christ. A mother once beautifully said, "I remember the new and strange emotions which trembled in my breast when as an infant he was first folded to my heart—my first-born child. The thrill of that moment still lingers; but when he was 'born again,' clasped in my arms a 'new creature in Christ Jesus,' my spiritual child, my son in the gospel, pardoned, justified, adopted, saved, for ever saved! Oh! it was the very depth of joy; joy unspeakable! My child was a child of God! The prayers which preceded his birth, which cradled his infancy, which girdled his youth, were answered. My son was Christ's. The weary watchings, the yearning desires, the trembling hopes of years were at rest. Our first-born son was avowedly the Lord's." May every father and mother here know just such joy by having sympathy with God.

But they had sympathy with *the son*. I am sure they rejoiced to see *him* back again, for somehow usually even bad sons have the goodwill of good servants. When young men go away, and are a great grief to their fathers, the servants often stick to them. They will say, "Well, Master John was very inconsiderate and gay, and he vexed his father a great deal, but I should like to see the poor boy back again." Especially is this true of the old servants who have been in the house since the boy was born: they never forget him. And you will find that God's old servants are always glad when they see prodigal children return; they are delighted beyond measure, because they love them after all, notwithstanding their wanderings. Sinner, with all your faults and hardness of heart we do love you, and we should be glad for your sake to see you delivered from eternal ruin and from the wrath of God which now abideth on you, and brought to rejoice in pardoned sin, and acceptance in the Beloved.

We should rejoice for the sinner's sake, but I think the servants rejoiced most of all when *they were the instruments* in the father's hand of blessing the son. Just look at this. The father said to the servants, "Bring forth the best robe." He might have gone to the wardrobe himself with a key and opened it, and brought out the robe himself, but he gave them the pleasure of doing it. When I get my orders from my Lord and Master on the Lord's-day morning to bring forth the best robe, I am delighted indeed. Nothing delights me more than to preach the imputed righteousness of Jesus Christ, and the substitutionary sacrifice of our exalted Redeemer. "Bring forth the best robe." Why, my Master, I might be content to keep out of heaven if thou wouldst always give me this work to do—to bring forth the best robe and extol and exalt Jesus Christ in the eyes of the people. Then he said, "Put it on him." When our Lord gives us grace to do that there is more joy still. How many times I have brought forth the best robe, but could not put it on you. I have held it up, and expatiated on its excellencies, and pointed to your rags, and said what a delightful thing it would be if I could put it on you, but I could not; but when the heavenly Father, by his divine grace and the power of the Spirit, makes us the means of bringing these treasures into the possession of poor sinners, oh, what joy! I should rejoice to bring forth the ring of the Spirit's sealing work, and the shoes of the preparation of the gospel of peace, for it is a joy to exhibit these blessings, and a greater joy still to put them upon the poor, returning wanderer. God be thanked for giving his servants so great a pleasure! I would not have dared to describe the Lord's servants as putting on the robe, the ring, and the shoes, but as he has himself done so I am rejoiced to use the Holy Spirit's own language.

How sweet was the command, "Put it on *him*." Yes, put it on the poor trembling, ragged, shivering sinner, "Put it on *him*," even on him, though he can hardly believe such mercy to be possible. "Put it on *him?*" Yes, on *him*. He who was a drunkard, a swearer, an adulterer? Yes, put it on *him*, for he repents. What joy it is when we are enabled by God's commission to throw that glorious mantle over a great sinner. As for the ring, put it on *him;* that is the beauty of it. And the shoes, put them on *him;* that they are for him is the essence of our joy—that such a sinner, and especially when he is one of our own household, should receive these gifts of grace is wonderful! It was most kind of the father to divide the labour of love. One would put on the robe, another the ring, and a third the shoes. Some of my brethren can preach Jesus Christ in his righteousness gloriously, and they put on the best robe; others seem most gifted in dwelling upon the work of the Spirit of God, and they put on the ring: while yet another class are practical divines, and they put on the shoes. I do not mind which I have to do, if I may but have a part in helping to bring to poor sinners those matchless gifts of grace, which at infinite expense the Lord has prepared for those who come back to him. How glad those were who helped to dress him I cannot tell. Meanwhile, another servant was gone off out of doors to bring in the fatted calf, and perhaps two or three were engaged in killing and dressing it, while another was lighting a fire in the kitchen, and preparing the spits for the roast. One laid the table, and another ran to the garden to bring flowers to make wreaths for the room,—I know I should have done that if I had been there. All were happy. All ready to join in the music and dancing. Those who work for the good of sinners are always the gladdest when they are saved. You who pray for them, you who teach them, you who preach to them, you who win them for Christ, you shall share their merriment.

Now, dear brethren, we are told that they "began to be merry," and according to the description it would seem that they were merry indeed, but still they only "began." I see no intimation that they ever left off. "They began to be merry," and as merriment is apt to grow beyond all bounds when it once starts, who knows what they have come to by this time. The saints begin to be merry now, and they will never cease, but rejoice evermore. On earth all the joy we have is only beginning to be merry, it is up in heaven that they get into full swing. Here our best delight is hardly better than a neap tide at its ebb; there the joy rolls along in the majesty of a full spring tide.

"Oh what rapturous hallelujahs
 In our Father's home above!
Hallelujah! Hallelujah!
 O'er the embraces of his love!
Wondrous welcome—God's own welcome,
May the chief of sinners prove.

"Sweet melodious strains ascending,
 All around a mighty flood;
Servants, friends, with joy attending—
 Oh! the happiness of God!
Grace abounding, all transcending,
Through a Saviour's precious blood."

Let us begin to be merry this morning. But we cannot unless we are labouring for the salvation of others in all ways possible to us. If we have done and are doing that, let us praise and bless the Lord, and rejoice with the reclaimed ones, and let us keep the feast as Jesus would have it kept; for I hope there is no one here of the elder brethren who will be angry and refuse to go in. Let us continue to be merry as long as we live, because the lost are found and the dead are made alive. God grant you to be merry on this account world without end. Amen.

PORTION OF SCRIPTURE READ BEFORE SERMON—Luke xv. 11—32.

www.ingramcontent.com/pod-product-compliance
Lightning Source LLC
LaVergne TN
LVHW021418110826
845150LV00007B/1982

* 9 7 8 1 4 2 5 5 0 9 5 9 0 *